Glynn Thomas

East Anglia A Different Perspective

Alan Marshall

First published in Great Britain in 2012 by Mascot Media Ltd, Norfolk, UK.
E-mail: mascot_media@btinternet.com
www.mascotmedia.co.uk

Revised second edition 2013

Illustrations © Glynn Thomas, photographed by David Burton.
www.glynnthomas.com

A CIP catalogue record for this book is available from the British Library.

ISBN: 978-0-9571811-2-0

All images from Glynn Thomas, or other sources as identified.

Designed by Ceri and Dan Thomas. Edited by Marion Scott Marshall.

Printed by Henry Ling Ltd, 23 High East Street, Dorchester, Dorset DT1 1HD.
E-mail: enquiries@henryling.co.uk

DEDICATIONS

Many thanks to Glynn and his family for their full support in this
venture. And to Marion for her constant encouragement.

Alan Marshall

I would like to dedicate this book to my grandchildren,
Hugh, Leo, Milo and Alice – all budding artists.

Glynn Thomas

Front cover (see also page 31) **Flatford** *2012 – 33 cm diameter*

Contents

⌃ **Crabbing**
2002 – 12 x 7 cm

Each year from 1982 to 2010 in the Suffolk coastal village of Walberswick, the British Open Crabbing Championship was held, raising funds for local, county and sea-related charities. In 2009 there was record attendance of 1,252 entrants, putting the event at risk as the small settlement on the banks of the River Blyth struggles to accommodate such numbers. Children and their accompanying adults still love to dangle smelly bait into the river in the hope of landing a champion crustacean.

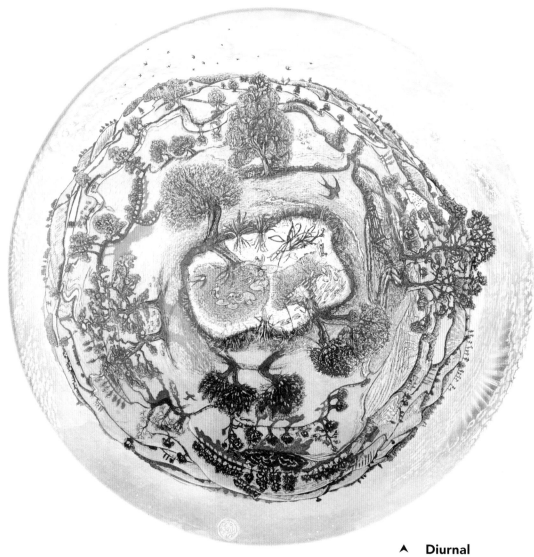

Scene Around

by Glynn Thomas RE

Born in Cambridge and based in Suffolk for more than 40 years, I have lived in East Anglia all my life. It is therefore only natural that the area's lovely coastline, charming villages, historic buildings and natural beauty should have inspired so much of my work.

It has long been a dream to produce a book of my work, but having self-published my Nepal Journal I was aware of how much time, energy and dedication would be needed to fulfill such a project. This book would never have come about without Alan and Marion suggesting it and making it possible. They have collated a retrospective 'exhibition' of images from the very early days up to the present. Thank you both for your commitment to the project, your patience and organisational skills.

My thanks go to all the galleries I have dealt with, and the patrons of my work, who have given me the opportunity to be a full-time artist since 1979.

I am very fortunate to have a 'right-hand-man', namely my wife, Pearl, who has tried to organise a disorganised printmaker: she frames the prints, keeps track of multiple deliveries to galleries, and looks after the accounts. My thanks for everything. Gallery owners often comment on how well organised I am!

Finally, there are two more people to whom I am indebted: my sons Ceri and Dan, who have been responsible for the design of this book and for my brilliant website. They are always on hand to produce excellent exhibition posters and pamphlets. Thank you both.

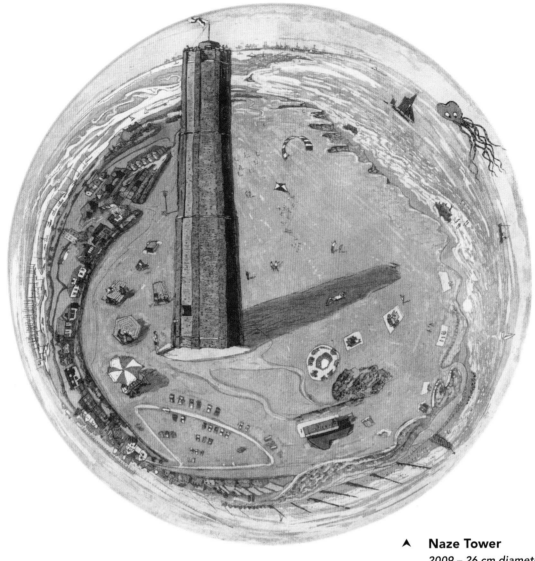

▲ **Naze Tower**
2009 – 26 cm diameter

Foreword

*by **Richard Bawden** RWS NEAC RE*

It always gives me great pleasure to see an etching by Glynn hanging on a wall in a friend's house or in an exhibition. I am always drawn into looking at it more closely. There is just so much to see. He is an exceptional draughtsman. He also has an eye. An eye that is observant; that distils the essence of a place and its character; and that captures the idiosyncratic.

The seaside, birds, boats, odd buildings and people crowding a busy beach; he has sketchbooks full of direct line drawings from which he works and from wherever he goes – not just East Anglia, but Venice and Nepal. His imagination takes him up into the sky where he sits on a cloud with a sketchbook and swivels around on his bottom to produce a circular panorama where the roads and waterways twist and turn like ribbons.

He has a surreal imagination that comes to the fore in his etching. The Naze Tower at Walton-on-the-Naze is a striking example of this; the tall brick structure with a long shadow across the cliff-top. The spirit of the place with the St George's flag, distilled into this dominant pillar.

Glynn was a student at Cambridge School of Art where he was taught printmaking by Walter Hoyle, in the St Barnabas annexe. This is where he found etching to be his medium. Walter was a taskmaster, having himself been taught by Edward Bawden, whom I know to have been a strict disciplinarian! Glynn puts a lot into his work and a lot comes out.

◀ **Margaret Catchpole's Cottage**
1969 – 10 x 15 cm
Glynn's first home in Suffolk

The Fine Print

Like many of his intricate and quirky etchings, Glynn David Laurie Thomas is an East Anglian original. Born in Cambridge and educated there during the height of 1960s creativity, Glynn moved to Suffolk in 1968 and has been one of the county's resident printmakers for more than 40 years, charming people with his offbeat interpretations of their favourite places. He uses ancient techniques and materials to put a fresh spin on the familiar, creating something new and thought-provoking.

This book gathers together for the first time an abbreviated history in words and pictures of the artist and his work – Glynn has been too prolific for a comprehensive catalogue of his output since leaving Cambridge School of Art in the late 1960s. During that time, he has passed on his skill and enthusiasm through teaching, picked up prestigious prizes, and helped fight worthy causes.

Travel has broadened his horizons and expanded his portfolio to include more exotic locations. While the original brief for this book was to expose the breadth and depth of his 'local' knowledge, Glynn has taken the opportunity to showcase some of his favourite 'foreign' subjects.

His choice to produce prints from etchings was a bold one. While his preferred medium dates back centuries, it had long ago fallen from grace. Once practised by Rembrandt, Goya and Whistler, etching had been sidelined by quicker, simpler and more contemporary printmaking methods such as screen-printing, linocuts and lithographs.

Glynn has dragged the neglected intaglio technique into the 21st century, using it to create instantly recognisable and highly desirable images that are thoroughly modern, but bring with them a comforting sense of history.

The front cover, for example, shows that there is far more to Flatford than just Constable. In typical Thomas style, Glynn explodes and reassembles a much-loved landscape to great effect, making us all stop, look and think again about buildings and scenery we've seen endless times, but never appreciated fully.

From Norfolk nature and windmills, via Cambridge colleges and Suffolk streets, to Essex estuaries and harbours, this is an unforgettable journey through the four counties of East Anglia and beyond.

 You may think you know these places well, but once you've viewed them from Glynn's 'different perspective' they will never look the same again "

And, no matter how often you turn the pages, there will always be something you missed last time around.

You may think you know these places well, but once you've viewed them from Glynn's 'different perspective' they will never look the same again.

Alan Marshall,
Norfolk, July 2012

A Different Perspective

Cambridge in 1946 was a very different place to the large, wealthy and cosmopolitan city we know today. Excluding some 30,000 students, the city is currently home to approximately 126,000 people. At the time of Glynn's birth, there were barely 80,000 residents, with World War II having played its tragic part in reducing the adult population.

Exhibiting himself for the first time on 7 April, exactly three months after future classmate Syd Barrett of Pink Floyd fame made his debut, Glynn was from a working-class background that might seem at odds with his eventual training in the Arts and a career first in education and later in printmaking.

The spot where Glynn grew up, as the son of a 'saw doctor' (a sawmill specialist who sharpens and services saw blades) and wood machinist, was very close to the River Cam and just a short bicycle ride from the city's surrounding countryside. Today, pedal bikes are the most fashionable means of transport in Cambridge. Back then, they were virtually the only choice for working people. In Glynn's street, there was just the one car — and it was a taxi cab. He observes that, today, you would be lucky to find a parking space for one car!

The streets around Glynn's home were his playground, including nearby Midsummer Common and Jesus Green. The latter is a park in central Cambridge, north of Jesus College, with the Cam running along the northern edge. To the east of Jesus Green is Victoria Avenue and, beyond that, Midsummer Common — land that is still used for grazing. Nowadays this is very desirable and valuable real estate. In the late 1940s and early 1950s, it was a simply a great environment for a growing boy.

At the age of 10, Glynn had a very traumatic and potentially life-changing accident. After a Cambridge City football match, he crushed his left hand in a large car park gate at the grounds. The aforementioned taxi now proved its worth by rushing him to the local hospital's Accident and Emergency department. Glynn was born left handed, so he — and the art world — were very lucky that the doctors were able to repair the damage.

Nature lover

Although primarily a town child, Glynn was encouraged by his father to show an interest in the countryside and nature. This was to stand him in good stead later in life, and not only for the influence of plant and animal life on his work. In addition to their small garden, the Thomas family had an allotment that was to kindle Glynn's life-long enthusiasm for vegetable growing. To this day, he devotes as much time as possible to growing his own organic food.

During the austere, post-war years of the early 1950s, holidays were scarce and a real luxury. Glynn remembers visits to a caravan on the North Norfolk coast, staying near Weybourne and East Runton off the coast road heading west from Cromer. A few years later, he recalls hitchhiking to Scotland, and once touring Ireland by motorcycle, with a tent for accommodation.

The main memories of his Cambridge childhood are happy ones, with plenty of play and not too much homework. One day at school he was told he was sitting something called 'the 11-plus', an exam created in 1944 that determined whether a pupil could attend grammar school or a less prestigious secondary modern. While Glynn was disappointed to fail, he found himself in the top form of Chesterton Secondary School, where practical skills and problem-solving formed part of the curriculum.

As it turned out, the failed exam and 'second prize' of a place at Chesterton proved to be a positive development. Glynn was taken under the wing of Art Master David Ashpole, who recognised Glynn's potential with the pencil and nurtured it. He is remembered fondly as an inspiring teacher, covering many aspects of art. Glynn became an enthusiastic student. During lunch

Glynn aged eight on a rare holiday in East Runton, Norfolk

and after school, he could generally be found involved in some art project or other.

It was David Ashpole who encouraged Glynn in 1962 to apply for a place at the well-regarded Cambridge Art School. Some 23 years after leaving Chesterton, Glynn would be invited to attend its golden jubilee celebrations, and was proud to have his work reproduced in a celebratory publication.

Taking to the water

Away from artistic pursuits, Glynn helped his father build a canoe. At the grand launch on the Cam, his father insisted on being the first to board the boat. He then proceeded to capsize not once, but twice. This didn't deter the young Glynn, who had many adventures with the canoe, including a 100-mile river and camping trip down the Wye.

He later became a successful oarsman for the school rowing eight, and then moved on to the famous Cambridge '99 Rowing Club, where he was stroke when the crew was successful in 'gaining its oars' in the 1962 Bumps. The club's motto has always stuck with him: "Success is labour's reward". Glynn's crew took part in a number of regattas, as well as the 31-mile Boston Rowing Marathon.

To supplement his pocket money (and, later, student grant), Glynn had many temporary and part-time jobs. His first paid art work was undertaken while at primary school and appeared in the local butcher's window. He painted, in whitewash, pigs and chickens, as well as lettering on the window.

Like many less wealthy schoolboys and students, Glynn did the rounds of casual work. He was a milkman's assistant (with horse!); grocery delivery boy, with bike; had a newspaper round; sold ice cream on Cambridge Railway Station; unloaded timber at the railway sidings; became a bus conductor; and worked on a number of building sites. The training here was put to good use in later years, when Glynn's Suffolk house required extensive work and he couldn't afford to hire professional workmen.

Thanks to the encouragement of

Proud to be a 'leftie': Glynn pictured in 1964

the aforementioned David Ashpole at Chesterton, Glynn applied for and won a place on a two-year foundation course at Cambridge Art School. He was very fortunate to have the blessing of his parents, who were happy to see him attending art school rather than getting a 'real' job. Glynn then derived income from waiting on tables at the various Cambridge colleges, where the 'serious' scholars were to be found.

In his element

For Glynn, however, the Art School was the perfect place to be, and he found himself in his element. The two years allowed time for students to assess their options and future artistic direction. The course covered a very wide range of art-related subjects, but drawing and observation – 'seeing', as Glynn puts it – were held in particularly high regard. Given how important this ability is for his work, the course was clearly a major influence on his career development.

The original Cambridge School of Art was founded in 1858 by renowned

'Sight.
Not a slight thing to teach, this: perhaps, on the whole, the most important thing to be taught in the whole range of teaching. To be taught to read – what is the use of that, if you know not whether what you read is false or true? To be taught to write or to speak – but what is the use of speaking, if you have nothing to say? To be taught to think – nay, what is the use of being able to think, if you have nothing to think of? But to be taught to see is to gain word and thought at once, and both true.'

Part of John Ruskin's inaugural address to the Cambridge Art School, 29 October 1858

Glynn (in Union Flag shirt) with Pearl on the student's Rag Week float in 1965. David Gilmour, later of Pink Floyd, is perched top left

British art patron, draughtsman, watercolourist and prominent social thinker John Ruskin. It was to be renamed Cambridgeshire College of Arts and Technology, and today forms part of Anglia Ruskin University.

During the highly creative and experimental 1960s, the School played host to many talented tutors and gifted students. They included caricaturists Roger Law and Peter Fluck, who gained notoriety at the Cambridge school and lasting fame in 1984 when their 'Spitting Image' puppets lampooned everyone from the Royal Family to politicians and musicians. No doubt the duo's taste for satire was helped by their friendship with comedian Peter Cook, who was to employ Law as an illustrator for 'Private Eye'. Law is today a ceramics designer, working with pottery and porcelain factories in China. Fluck works full time as an artist, living in a remote part of Cornwall with his painter wife Anne-Cecile de Bruyne.

An earlier and still higher-profile alumnus of the Cambridge School was legendary cartoonist and graphic artist Ronald Searle, who died in 2012 and seems destined to be remembered more

for his St Trinian's characters than for any other achievement during seven decades of ground-breaking work.

Still more influential in terms of Glynn's eventual career was Edward Bawden, who studied at the Cambridge School of Art in 1919–1921. Bawden was one of Britain's greatest graphic artists, illustrators and printmakers. Glynn was honoured later in life to see his work hanging alongside that of Bawden – and counts Edward's son Richard as a personal friend and printmaking contemporary. Indeed, Richard Bawden has provided the foreword to this book, describing Glynn as "an exceptional draughtsman" with an eye that "distils the essence of a place and its character and captures the idiosyncratic".

Memories of Syd

Glynn, having moved straight from his two foundation years to a three-year degree course, was to be at the Cambridge School of Art until 1967 and to rub shoulders with luminaries such as Pink Floyd founder member, the late Roger (Syd) Barrett. Just three months older than Glynn, Barrett was a fine painter who found greater fame with a Fender Telecaster in his hands.

Starting in 1964, the band that would become Pink Floyd underwent various line-up and name changes such as 'The Abdabs', 'The Screaming Abdabs', 'Sigma 6' and 'The Meggadeaths'. In 1965, Barrett joined them as 'The Tea Set'. When encountering a band of the same name, Syd opted for 'The Pink Floyd Sound', which was later shortened to 'The Pink Floyd'.

One of the first gigs of the new band was at the Cambridge Art School Christmas party in December 1966. According to Glynn, the band projected slides daubed with oils and colours as a psychedelic light show. He recalls that the band was "incredibly loud" and that you couldn't hear the music properly unless you were a couple of studios away. Cambridge Art School student John Gordon (himself a budding musician) designed the tickets for the show, produced from a linocut. The price to attend? Seven shillings and sixpence.

Pink Floyd led, indirectly, to Glynn's

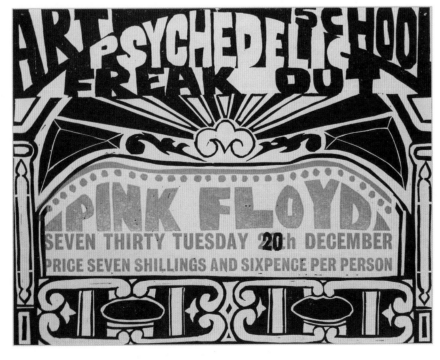

Fellow student and budding musician John Gordon's lino-printed ticket for the Art School's Christmas party, 1966

marriage. In October 1964, when he was 18, Glynn met his future wife Pearl at Cambridge hotspot Les Jeux Interdits (now Marks & Spencer!) where the band 'Jokers Wild' was making its debut. On guitar was future Pink Floyd frontman David Gilmour. Music was a big part of the 'scene' – Glynn remembers camping on the pavement overnight to get tickets to see the Beatles, and travelling great distances to watch the Rolling Stones.

While music was an entertaining distraction, there was serious business to attend to at the School. Glynn's chosen subjects for the degree course were illustration and printmaking. One of his tutors was Walter Hoyle, a close friend of Edward Bawden and an exceptional printmaker in his own right.

Under Walter's wing

Hoyle was born in Lancashire and studied at Beckenham School of Art from 1938. He then gained a place at the Royal College of Art (RCA) in 1940, where he learnt printmaking and other skills under Bawden. They became close friends and Hoyle later moved to the Essex village of Great Bardfield to live and work alongside Bawden.

He held many major exhibitions throughout his long career, and his work is in collections such as the Tate Gallery. He taught at Cambridge Art School from 1964 until retiring in 1985, placing great emphasis on printmaking.

Great Bardfield was to become the home of many prominent 20th-century English artists who hosted a series of 'open house' exhibitions in the village during the 1950s. These events garnered national press attention and attracted thousands of visitors.

The major artists of the 1940s and 1950s included John Aldridge, Edward Bawden, George Chapman, Stanley Clifford-Smith, Audrey Cruddas, Walter Hoyle, Michael Rothenstein, Eric Ravilious (who lodged with Bawden at Brick House), Sheila Robinson and Marianne Straub.

Other influential tutors at the Cambridge School included John Norris Wood, who had himself studied painting and illustration at London's

Goldsmith's College, and printmaking and illustration at the RCA, where he won the silver medal for zoological drawing. He became the driving force behind the Natural History Illustration and Ecological Studies programme at the RCA.

Painter, designer and teacher

∧ **Alphabet**
(compilation of linocuts, wood engravings, etchings and drawings printed as a screenprint)
1967 – 76 x 51 cm

and newspapers. A musician as well as an artist (he helped found the legendary Cambridge Folk Festival), he still works from his 17th-century studio near Cambridge.

Thanks to the tuition of Hoyle and his colleagues, Glynn was introduced to the work of the great printmaking masters, Rembrandt Harmenszoon van Rijn (Netherlands, 1606–1669), Francisco de Goya (Spain 1746–1828) and Britain's own Thomas Bewick (1753–1828). The printmaking course covered the major methods of wood-engraving, lino-cutting, lithography, screen-printing and etching. Glynn caught the bug, and began to consider a life based around printmaking.

Learning the alphabet

He lost himself in a multitude of different processes and learnt to love lithography and screen-printing. A major project was a large alphabet that used a wide range of methods including woodcuts, linoprints, etchings and screen-printing. Gaining experience in each of the key processes proved invaluable when Glynn began teaching in the early 1970s.

Students from the School designed and illustrated a number of promotional brochures, catalogues and publications, such as a guide for The Saffron Walden Museum Society. One such limited-edition booklet featured Glynn and five other first-year students, using a selection of popular printmaking techniques.

Among many notable achievements, Hoyle in 1964 founded the Cambridge Print Editions and organised joint exhibitions for students and professional artists at the Heffers Art Gallery and the Senate House in Cambridge.

The proceeds of any sales were divided three ways between the artist, funding for the School's printmaking materials, and working trips for students. One such was an artistic expedition to Paris. The exhibitions were a great success and provided a much needed incentive for the students, who could not only earn hard cash but could also enjoy foreign travel.

∧ **Notre Dame de Paris (linoprint)**
1967 – 71 x 46 cm

John Bolam studied furniture design at High Wycombe School of Art, and went on to become Principal of the School of Art at Cambridge. Another of the teaching team, illustrator John Holder specialises in classic pen drawing with a humorous twist. His work has been seen in numerous books, magazines

Cambridge Print Editions had, by the mid-1960s, moved into new premises in St Barnabas Sunday School, off Mill Road in the city centre. At the time, this was arguably the best-equipped print shop of its kind outside London.

The summer of 1966 saw some of the Cambridge students heading for Paris to make contact with galleries and sell their prints. This was the first such expedition, and Glynn was one of the chosen few. He produced a complex linoprint of Notre Dame Cathedral.

At the May 1967 exhibition at the Senate House, Glynn's Notre Dame print was one of those offered for sale, priced at nine guineas. It was on show with his prints of King's College Cambridge and Grantchester, as well as his alphabet piece that had been created using a variety of printmaking techniques. Also selling at the show were works by Edward Bawden, Bill Darrell, George Chapman, Walter Hoyle, Paul Beck and John Bolam.

Apart from the pleasure of selling prints and the prospect of foreign travel, the ultimate accolade of exhibiting, according to Glynn, was to be allowed to appear alongside Edward Bawden and other long-established and highly regarded artists. He describes it as a "huge thrill", but also as a "great responsibility". Having work on display alongside great artists means that there is tremendous pressure to produce your best work.

The artistic life

For Glynn, interest in his early drawings and prints sparked the idea that he might be able to make a living from his art. It took a while, but he was ultimately proved right. However, in his final year at Cambridge School of Art, Glynn considered the option of part-time teaching and freelance illustration. A number of commissions were achieved including a pictorial book on Victorian Cambridge and images used in poetry volumes and for book covers.

'Victorian Cambridge', published in 1969 and costing 21 shillings, was illustrated throughout by Glynn's whimsical drawings of sportsmen, entertainers, events and places. It

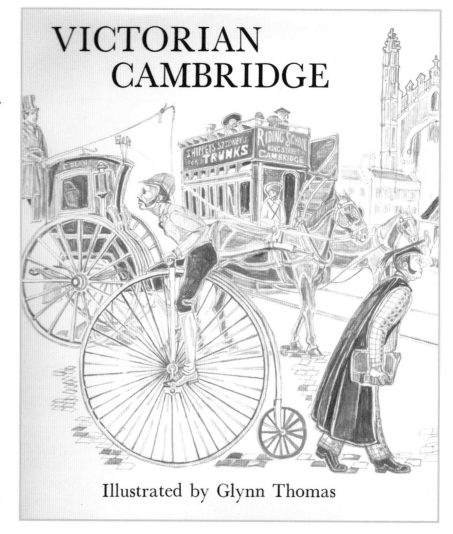

Two book covers from 1969. Left: 'Victorian Cambridge', illustrated throughout by Glynn; and, below, Geoffrey Grigson's 'A Choice of Thomas Hardy's Poems'

Aldeburgh Fisherman
1975 – 16 x 12 cm

Weekend
1975 – 29 x 20 cm

was based on work produced while on his degree course, which was then expanded into a quaint stand-alone publication.

Glynn's artwork graced the cover of the 1969 Geoffrey Grigson book 'A Choice of Thomas Hardy's Poems', produced as a three-colour linoprint. The book also featured a number of Glynn's etchings and linoprints. The same author in 1971 used Glynn's work for the cover and run-of-book illustrations for 'Rainbows, Fleas and Flowers'.

On graduating from art school in 1967, Glynn hoped to land a part-time teaching position that would provide steady income, but allow him time to develop his printmaking and illustration. Instead, he was offered a full-time post at the Ipswich Civic College School of Art in Suffolk alongside the likes of Colin Moss and Bernard Reynolds. It meant a move away from Cambridge and the postponement of plans for a career as an artist. It was also too good an opportunity to turn down, particularly as Glynn and Pearl had married in Melbourn (south Cambridgeshire) in 1966 and were looking to set up home.

Glynn became senior lecturer in charge of the printmaking department at the Ipswich school, dealing mainly with students on the art & design foundation course. He was to remain at the institution for 11 years. During this time he was able to use the department's facilities in the evenings and build up a portfolio of work — sufficient for an exhibition.

Ipswich had already established an enviable reputation for producing exciting young artists who then went on to more distinguished art schools such as the Slade, while many of the tutors were also working artists who had experienced success in their respective fields.

The school administration was later to state that Glynn had shown from the outset "an unusual capacity for helping students to develop their individual potential as artists". The use of various printmaking media allowed successive groups to produce "a rich variety of interesting prints of quality".

Regular work and pay meant Glynn and Pearl could find a home and start a family, with first son Ceri born in 1969, a year after the move to Suffolk. Dan would make his first appearance two years later, once they had moved into their new house at Capel St Mary.

Glynn in 1974 became a member of the Society of Industrial Artists and Designers. Later that year, he discussed his desire for a dedicated show with Ipswich picture restorer Mike Swinyard, hoping it would help launch his career as a professional printmaker.

Mike immediately offered Glynn space for a one-man exhibition at the St Lawrence Gallery in Dial Lane, Ipswich. While this may not have been Glynn's first solo event, having in 1973 shown his work at the Cambridge Arts Theatre and Framlingham Art Gallery, it was to be the first serious selling opportunity for his new etchings. Few had yet seen the unique approach Glynn was taking to recreating familiar scenes in an unfamiliar way.

Having recognised the limitations of conventional perspective drawings, which invariably omit much of what can be captured by the human eye, he had developed a technique for showing much more of a village or landscape by redistributing the buildings and landmarks, often using curves or even circles to accommodate as much of the location as possible.

The method of printmaking chosen by Glynn reflects the highly illustrative nature of his work, which could not be achieved using the other major processes. With etching, he is able to obtain the fine detail that helps make his work stand out from the crowd.

First show

The catalogue from this breakthrough show lists 37 etchings, only a couple of which (such as the Grantchester prints from his Cambridge days) had appeared in previous exhibitions. Many of the new pieces depicted familiar Suffolk locations such as Pin Mill, Aldeburgh and Kersey. Prices ranged from £4 unframed to a princely £23 framed.

The public warmed to the unusual and appealing selection of work. The event was extremely successful and

generated enough funds (more than £1,000) for Glynn to buy his own Harry Rochat etching press.

Engineering firm Harry Rochat is still in existence, operating out of High Barnet in Hertfordshire and supplying highest-quality fine art etching, Albion, direct and offset litho presses and associated equipment. The firm was started in 1969 by Harry Rochat and his son Leon. The castings for their presses are produced by a family-run foundry in Birmingham, then machined and finished in the small factory in Barnet.

During the previous year, Glynn had drawn up plans for a double-storey extension, including studio, to his elderly house in Capel St Mary, which he proceeded to build himself with the minimum of help. He therefore had a suitable home for his new press and the incentive to make final plans to abandon teaching.

Planning his future

Given the scale and nature of the proposed building project, Glynn's skills as a draughtsman came in very useful. His drawings for the extension, fortunately, were conventional, rather than showing elements of his home exploded and redistributed in circular form!

He completed the plans and had them checked and okayed by a friend who was a clerk of the works. Seeking to minimise costs, he began scrounging free building materials. A church near the Ipswich art school premises was being demolished. Glynn took his old van during his lunch break and hauled away anything he thought he could use. All the timber and doors in the extension came from the abandoned church. He reckons that he spent no more than £600 on that particular extension, thanks to his successful scavenging.

Also in Ipswich, a large Victorian building was being taken down to make room for the new Willis insurance offices. Glynn wanted the tiles being removed from the site, but didn't have much money to spare. He approached the site foreman who explained that if his team removed the tiles, they would have to charge £25 per 1,000. If Glynn did the work himself, it would cost just £5.

The tiles were located four floors up, but Glynn didn't hesitate to confront the challenge. In a single day, he removed 1,500 tiles, carrying them down the four flights of stairs, loading them into the van, driving them back to Capel St Mary, then unloading them ready for use in his home. He remembers being fit for nothing the following day …

Confidence booster

With building work more or less complete and the studio up and running, he became still more determined to establish himself as a professional artist. Helping his confidence and credibility was the

The letter confirming Glynn's membership of the Royal Society of Painter-Etchers and Engravers (RSE, now the RE)

▼ St Mary's Maldon
1979 – 11 x 17 cm

January 1976 decision by the Royal Society of Painter-Etchers and Engravers (RSE, now the RE) to elect Glynn as an Associate Member of the Society – his name had been put forward by Charles Bartlett, who later became President of the RSE.

The Society dates back to 1884, and at that time had 150 members including the great and the good of British printmaking. It was formed to fight the cause of neglected and underrated intaglio artists, helping to raise their profile and standing in artistic society.

The same year saw a different kind of recognition, as Glynn's work appeared for the first time on the walls of the Royal Academy in London as part of the annual Summer Exhibition.

More one-man shows were organised in the wake of the breakthrough Ipswich exhibition, with Glynn still fitting in the etching and printmaking with his teaching commitments. September 1977 saw the first of many exhibitions in the Essex town of Colchester, at The Craftsman in Trinity Street. Wivenhoe, Thaxted, Dedham, Felixstowe Ferry, Flatford, Mersea Island and Ellingham Mill were among the familiar local scenes featured at the gallery.

Eaton House Publishers was by then selling Glynn's prints in New York through its US parent, with images of Wivenhoe, Thaxted and Flatford catching the eye of exhibition attendees at Adelphi University.

Glynn had begun to support local appeals and charitable causes, something that would remain part of his life and work. An edition of 75 prints was made of his Maldon Hythe Quay etching, which showcased the ailing St Mary's church tower and was sold to help raise money for essential repairs. A year later he was backing the same town's Two Towers appeal that had brought the crumbling St Peter's Tower to public attention.

The initial St Mary's edition was commissioned by Mrs Anstice Shaw of Maldon, who at the time ran the Minories Art Gallery in Colchester. The sale of the prints was to help contribute to a fund for the repair of the old quayside church tower. Glynn's etching was on show at three places in Maldon, and the fund ultimately benefited to the tune of £740.

Thanks to the success of the project, a new coloured print providing a 'bird's eye' view of St Peter's Tower at Maldon was commissioned and offered for sale from December 1979. The aim was to raise £825 for the Two Towers appeal. Glynn has gone on to produce various prints over a number of years for worthy local causes, with the most recent being 'Free the Quay' in the Essex village of Mistley.

In May 1983, St Mary's of Maldon benefited once more from Glynn's efforts. The church restoration fund held an exhibition of 30 coloured etchings, with a share of the proceeds from a new Maldon print heading into the fund's coffers.

Taking the plunge

By 1979, it was time for Glynn to make the break from teaching and commit fully to his art. With the well-equipped studio at home, the support of Pearl and the growing popularity of his work, he tendered his resignation – and finally got the offer of part-time work he had been seeking a decade earlier! He spent a final six months at the Ipswich institution on a limited-hours basis, before casting himself adrift with his imagination and his press.

Another memorable event of 1979 was the arrival on the Glynn Thomas scene of the influential Christie's Contemporary Art (CCA), a subsidiary of the world-famous auction house, Christie's International.

Founded in 1972, CCA helped to establish original prints as a major art form in their own right, and as a way of collecting genuine high-quality art at an affordable price. The aim of the organisation was to seek out and publish the best prints available by famous and established printmakers, as well as young artists in the early stages of their careers. Even though he was then aged 33, Glynn still qualified as one of the latter.

The Dover Street-based CCA was quick to recognise the appeal of Glynn's highly original work, which had the added merit of exploiting a very traditional and chronically under-used technique. 'Along the Stour' and 'Opposite Banks of the Stour' were commissioned in 1979 and received with great enthusiasm. By May of that year, CCA was writing to ask for more copies, as 'Along the Stour' was "going particularly well". The editions were of 150 prints, each signed and numbered.

Glynn recalls that CCA had an insatiable appetite and would have taken virtually everything he could produce, using up all his time and effort. Between 1980 and 1982 he provided the gallery with 'Dedham Vale', 'Suffolk Meadow', 'Reedmace' and 'Yellow Iris', again in editions of 150.

Now working full time as an artist, Glynn began a relentless programme of creating new etchings and selling his prints through an expanding network of galleries. Shows were held in Northamptonshire and Gloucestershire, as well as in Colchester (at the Minories Art Gallery), at Manchester's Corn Exchange and in Ipswich.

His work was shown alongside that of other leading printmakers at the prestigious Bankside Gallery in London, where an etching of a Normandy port caught the eye of visitors. 'Honfleur' was judged to be the best of more than 300 entries in a competition staged by the gallery. Glynn

had made preliminary sketches when on holiday in France a couple of years earlier, and was pleasantly surprised that a 'foreign' subject would attract such great acclaim.

London has not only inspired some of Glynn's most popular work, but its galleries have been very supportive. A 1995 foyer exhibit at the Barbican Centre not only drew great praise and effusive thanks from the organisers, but led to his work being hung in The Museum of London after its art curator, Mirielle Gallinou, viewed the prints at The Barbican.

June 2008 saw the Parliamentary Art Collection in Westminster select four of Glynn's prints for inclusion among 7,000 works dating from medieval times to the present day. The choices were 'Cromer', 'Maritime Ipswich', 'Cambridge' and 'Cambridge Courts' — all of which can be found in this book.

Glowing review

'The Guardian' in 1983 helped boost Glynn's national reputation by publishing a glowing review of his work. Ray Rushton described the etchings as "intriguing and inventive". He talked of Glynn ignoring formal perspective, "switching and changing his viewpoint" to interlock his composition of architectural minutiae and other items of potted civic biography "like a flatearther producing a map of the known world".

Given Glynn's obvious fascination with the aerial perspective, it is no surprise that he would love to be able to fly. Over the years he has made great efforts to gain access to high vantage points when preparing for a new work. His vertical journeys have included King's College Chapel, Cambridge University Library, St Paul's Cathedral, Canary Wharf, Tower Bridge, The London Eye, Guy's Hospital, Orfordness and Southwold lighthouses, Bircham Windmill and many others. There have been two trips in hot air balloons and a light aircraft flight over Suffolk and Essex. In recent years, internet-based application Google Earth has been of great assistance. The aerial views are no replacement for a site visit, but can augment his notes and

Glynn Thomas

"Dedham Vale"

Original etching and aquatint
1 plate, 6 colours
Printed by the artist on
R K Burt paper.
Edition size 150, signed and
numbered.
Paper size: 20" × 25"
(51 cm × 63 cm).
Image size: 11" × 14"
(28 cm × 35 cm).

Glynn Thomas was born in
Cambridge in 1946 and studied
at the Cambridge School of Art.
He was elected an associate
member of the Royal Society of
Etchers and Engravers in 1976;
and in the same year exhibited at
the Royal Academy. His work is
in various public and private
collections throughout the world.

Christie's Contemporary Art

Glynn Thomas

"Suffolk Meadow"

Original etching and aquatint
1 plate, 4 colours
Printed by the artist on
R K Burt paper.
Edition size 150, signed and
numbered.
Paper size: 20" × 25"
(51 cm × 63 cm).
Image size: 11" × 14"
(28 cm × 35 cm).

Glynn Thomas was born in
Cambridge in 1946 and studied
at the Cambridge School of Art.
He was elected an associate
member of the Royal Society of
Etchers and Engravers in 1976;
and in the same year exhibited at
the Royal Academy. His work is
in various public and private
collections throughout the world.

Christie's Contemporary Art

Christie's Contemporary Art publicity, 1979

sketches by showing him more of the surrounding geography and perspective.

Observation and an eye for detail are at the heart of his work. "The more you look, the more you see." Good drawing is essential for good etching, so Glynn needs to capture accurately all that he sees. His technique may have been refined over the years but, essentially, his way of working and the subjects that appeal to him have remained largely unchanged.

Glynn works from life, not from books. He will take photographs on location to supplement his many detailed sketches and notes, particularly if the subject and planned etching is unusually complicated.

"The way I approach a subject is that I take the view that you are walking through a landscape. You start off with what is in front of you – then I draw what is beyond that and possibly behind me. I have a habit of layering things one on top of the other."

On developing his style, Glynn didn't want to be limited to the ordinary, restricted view. "Everybody draws things in rectangles, but if you close one eye you see your nose and the elliptical shape of the eye, so I was always intrigued by how each eye sees different things."

He admits that he has a particular affinity with the coast and with water in general. Many of his works are coastal scenes or have a river in them, including his London and Cambridge scenes. The famous view from the dome of St Paul's still finds room for the Thames to play an important role.

East Anglia — and beyond

The focus of this book may be on the four counties of East Anglia, which have provided a rich source of inspiration and hundreds of images, but the artist's eye never sleeps and Glynn's international travel has resulted in some outstanding work.

From Paris, Honfleur, Monpazier, Peillon and the Dordogne, to Provencal villages and St Leon sur Vezere, France has always been a popular destination for the Thomas family and is well represented in Glynn's portfolio.

In Italy, Venice was the perfect

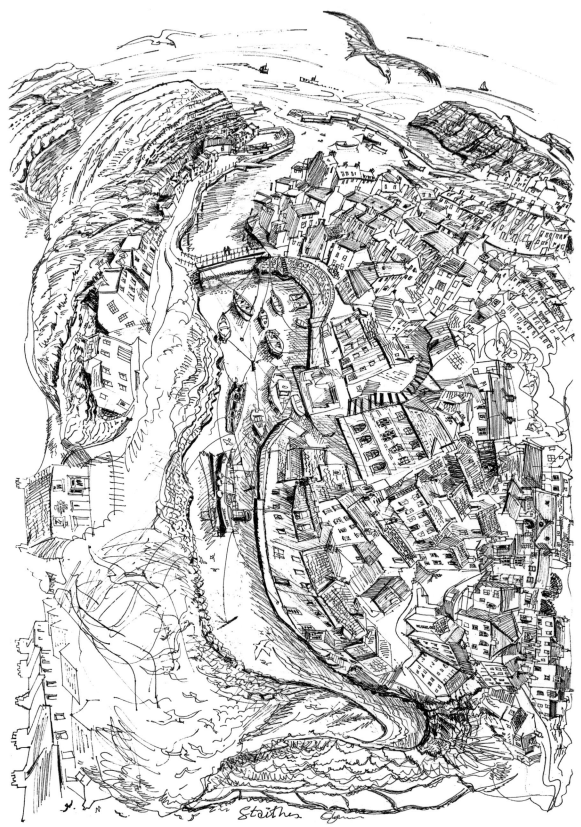

I feel very privileged to have attended Cambridge Art School in the 60s when drawing from observation was an important part of the curriculum.
This has been the foundation of all my working life —
it is said that seeing is believing; my belief is that drawing is seeing.

choice, and Glynn's unorthodox work provides a nice contrast to that of Canaletto. Rome, Capri, Siena, Pisa, San Gimignano and the Amalfi coast all received the Thomas treatment.

Glynn is probably the ideal artist to tackle Peru's mighty and mysterious Machu Picchu. Not many people get to look down on a 15th-century Inca stronghold that is found 2,400 metres up in the Andes!

You get a glimpse of the pyramids at Luxor in his depiction of Egyptian feluccas on the Nile, while a three-week expedition to Nepal in 1996 (to celebrate his 50th birthday) resulted in fantastic etchings of Durbar Square in Patan and the foothills of Annapurna. Observations, sketches and finished works can be found in a small, self-published book that provides a record of the adventure.

Putting pen to paper

When Glynn has chosen a subject for an etching, he will generally spend quite a long time absorbing the immediate area around it before putting pen to paper. In some instances, it may take a year or more before he feels ready to tackle the subject. Once he has all the required information he will decide on various compositions and also on the size of etching he believes the subject matter needs.

It is a very time-consuming process to produce an etching and the resulting limited-edition prints. From conception to creation, Glynn claims that his biggest etchings can take more than 200 hours of work.

Once he has the completed plate, it can take up to 45 minutes of inking up the colours in order to make just one print. As his editions are typically of 150 or 200 prints, in order to keep the selling cost at an affordable level he can devote up to 15 days' solid work on completing an edition of just one image! However, apart from the work for Christie's between 1979 and 1982, Glynn does not produce a whole edition in one go but gradually prints it over a number of years — mostly in the winter months.

Glynn's early work was carried out on zinc plates and mostly printed

A three-week expedition to Nepal in 1996 (to celebrate Glynn's 50th birthday) resulted in fantastic etchings of Durbar Square in Patan and the foothills of Annapurna – Glynn's notebook, containing observations, sketches and finished works, was subsequently published in a small edition that provides a record of his Nepalese adventure

in sepia. One reason was economy; another being that coloured printing is problematic on zinc, with chemical reactions changing some colours. Glynn now works exclusively with copper as it gives a much finer quality of work.

Each of Glynn's prints is signed by the artist, and the number of prints in an edition is written on the bottom left-hand side. Above this is the number of the particular print in that edition. An additional 10 per cent of an edition can be marked as 'artist's proof', which may be retained by the creator or sold.

It is important for Glynn and all professional printmakers that customers understand the process and appreciate the individuality of each finished piece. Glynn's Uncle Laurie was an engineer and, in his retirement, designed and produced to Glynn's specifications a small portable etching press that he can take to exhibitions.

During demonstrations in galleries, it amuses Glynn to hear the gasps of amazement when he pulls a print from the plate and displays it. He is asked regularly if he has to ink up the plate every time. On learning the answer, the audience begins to appreciate more fully the work and craftsmanship involved in the etching process. They also realise that the prints they are buying aren't just limited in number, but are very much originals and not copies.

Glynn's work isn't limited to buildings and landscapes. His lifelong interest in the natural world has resulted in a large number of prints featuring trees, plants, animals and birds. Cats are a familiar sight in many etchings, both as 'extras' in bigger works and as stars of their own prints. The Thomas household has provided a home for many grateful and pampered moggies, with a few preserved forever on copper plate.

Play Mistley for me …

During his early career, Glynn donated his time and talent to helping good causes, such as the St Mary's church tower appeal in Maldon. More recently, he has leapt to the defence of another Essex beauty spot.

In September 2008, the owners of the quayside in the village of Mistley erected a tall, unsightly and unpopular fence that ended 500 years of free access to the water. Parents and children were no longer able to feed the ever-hungry swans that form a major attraction at this pleasant spot, while visiting

Poster designed by Dan Thomas for Mistley's 'Free the Quay' promotional exhibition, 2012

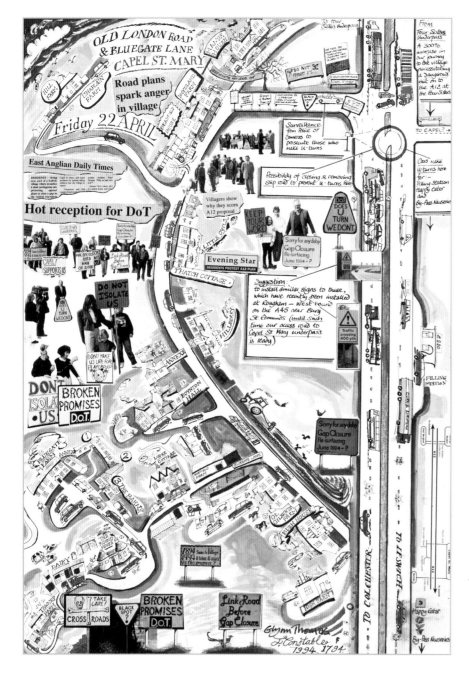

◄ **Road
Campaign
Poster**
*1994 –
120 x 70 cm*

the day — albeit almost six years later.

June 2004 saw the final go-ahead for the £800,000 road scheme, which resulted in a new link built between Old London Road and the Bentley Road, making it easier for motorists to join and leave the A12 east of Capel St Mary. The link road now runs from Bluegate Lane to Bentley Road, across land owned by Suffolk County Council. At the same time, the gap in the central reservation at the Pound Lane junction with the A12 was sealed to stop traffic crossing the busy trunk road to join the opposite side of the carriageway.

Few doubt that the sustained pressure put on the authorities over the entire period was critical to the outcome, and that the new measures will have saved lives as well as making life easier for residents.

Glynn was long ago absorbed into his Suffolk community, to the extent that most Thomas family members have become ardent Ipswich Town supporters. Woe betide any gallery trying to arrange a viewing on a Saturday when there is a home game!

Glynn has built up an enthusiastic 'fan base', with devotees buying prints on a regular basis, attending shows throughout East Anglia and keeping up with developments via his website. Pearl helps keep the business ticking over efficiently, framing prints for exhibitions and customers, as well as managing family affairs so that Glynn can devote enough time to running off prints, checking out locations and preparing fresh etchings.

His much extended house now has a viewing platform from which Glynn can enjoy the countryside around him. There is, of course, a well-tended vegetable garden to provide that 'Good Life' factor of at least partial food self-sufficiency.

Friends reunited

June 2007 saw former students from Glynn's art school days gather in Cambridge. Glynn helped organise the reunion and was pleased to find that so many of his contemporaries from the 1960s had achieved success.

Those attending the reunion from Glynn's three-year degree course

'twitchers' felt as though they were viewing caged birds.

A portion of sales proceeds from Glynn's most recent Mistley Quay print go to the 'Free the Quay' campaign. As this book went to press, there were signs that the local council might bring the fence affair to a satisfactory conclusion, and that Mistley Quay might be set free. Glynn is justifiably proud of his involvement.

Sometimes the causes can be closer to home. Residents of Old London Road in Capel St Mary (Glynn's home village) campaigned for more than 10 years in an attempt to get a road link

built that would connect them with the rest of the village, having been cut off by the increasingly busy and dangerous A12 dual carriageway. Glynn had worked with the campaigners, providing detailed drawings and publicity material to support the efforts of the Old London Road Residents' Association.

Victory appeared to have been achieved in 1998, when the route for the new link and the necessary budget were agreed. The government then slashed its road-building programme and the link was deemed to be "too expensive". The campaign was forced to start all over again and eventually won

June 2007 saw former students from Glynn's art school days gather in Cambridge. Glynn helped organise the reunion and was pleased to find that so many of his contemporaries from the 1960s had achieved success

included Richard Jacobs, a graphic designer, illustrator and lecturer. Richard had designed the pop-art float for the 1965 University Rag Day, which had won the 'London Evening Standard' prize for the best float.

John Gordon, previously an art director and illustrator, and now a Gold Star member of the Magic Circle, was present at the gathering. Also attending were well-known illustrator Pauline Ellison and her painter husband Poul Webb. Another successful artist at the reunion was Richard Neal, a Fenland painter of whimsical agricultural scenes.

Glynn and company were also joined by Ian Evans, a designer for 'Reader's Digest', and illustrator and musician John Watkins. Overall, plenty of talent that had clearly benefited from their Cambridge days. Absent, of course, was Syd Barrett, whose lonely life came to an end just a year before the reunion.

Putting Flatford through the mill

Long before this book was in the planning stage, Glynn had been approached by the management of the National Trust Boat House Gallery,

adjoining Flatford Mill, which was being used to mount exhibitions by largely local artists. Being the scene of Constable's finest hour, Glynn couldn't say no to a display of his work at such an artistically significant venue.

In March 2012, Suffolk was enjoying exceptionally good weather. With Flatford being just a couple of miles from Glynn's home, he was able to spend a rewarding month gathering material for the series of prints that appear in this book. In April he started working on the plates. As this was to be one of the wettest Aprils on record, his timing had proved to be perfect, in that he could devote several weeks in the studio to the four Flatford etchings.

The result of Glynn's visit to the heart of Constable Country graces the front cover and, once again, shows how familiar places can be transformed through an imaginative artist's eyes.

He is pleased that both of his sons, Ceri and Dan, have made careers in graphic design, inspired by their father's 'different perspective'. Their unstinting help with publicity and Glynn's website, as well as Ceri and Dan's role in the layout of this book, reflects a great respect for Glynn's work. ✵

Glynn printing the Flatford Mill plate (cover image and page 31)

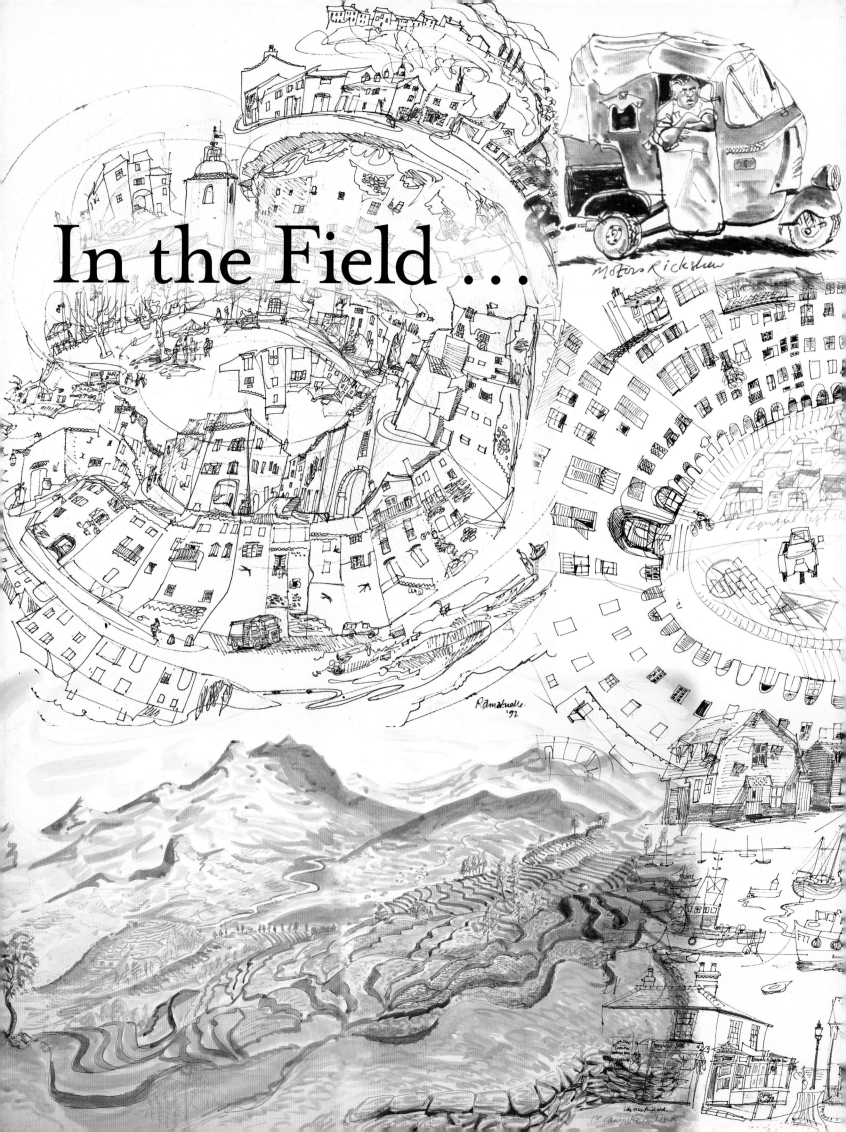

In the Field ...

...ul tells us about rafting - once a man was tossed from the back of the boat to the front and smashed his face onto a metal box. No doctor so they had to stitch his face without anaesthetic.

oar detail

dug out

Intaglio Etching

Printmaking method where the action of a roller press forces the paper into lines sunk beneath the surface of a metal plate, squeezing ink from them so that it stands out in slight relief from the paper. Etching, engraving, mezzotint and techniques such as drypoint are all intaglio processes.

Working drawing

Tracing

Drawing through wax ground

Line proof

Proof with aquatint

Aquatint plate with highlights painted out

Twenty seconds total in acid

Forty seconds total in acid

One minute total in acid

Two minutes total in acid

Four minutes total in acid

Two etching processes explained

Glynn drawing into the wax-covered copper plate with a needle

Line etching

The plate is covered with an acid-resist wax ground and the image is drawn through this on to the underlying copper with a fine needle. The longer the plate is immersed in the acid the deeper and darker the etched line will appear in the final print. A varnish is used to 'stop out' lines at various stages to prevent the acid from etching any further. N.B. The drawing on the plate is carried out in reverse – special care has to be taken with lettering!

Aquatint etching

An etching method that is very useful for colour printing as it enables the artist to achieve a wide range of colour tones. First, the plate is covered with a very fine powdered resin that is melted on the plate. Each resin dot is acid-resistant; therefore, the acid eats away the metal in between each dot.

If you look carefully at the test strip you can see the resin dots, which appear white. At the first stage the highlights are painted out with the stop-out varnish; it appears that one is working in negative. The plate is immersed in acid for a very short time to etch the first light tone, which is then retained by applying more varnish. This sequence continues until the last area is exposed to the acid for the longest time, which gives the darkest tone.

Line and aquatint etching test strips

The strips below show how long the plate was left in acid. It can be seen on the line etching test strip on the left that the original fine line has become wider and darker because of the width and depth of the acid 'bite'. The aquatint strip on the right shows how darker tones are achieved with a longer etching time.

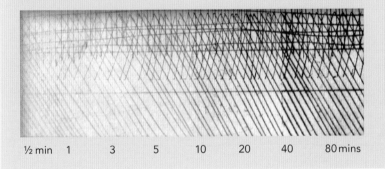

½ min   1   3   5   10   20   40   80 mins

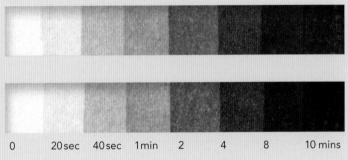

0   20 sec   40 sec   1 min   2   4   8   10 mins

 Six minutes total in acid

Eight minutes total in acid

Ten minutes total in acid

Inked-up coloured plate – all colours applied on the one plate

Finished etching of Willy Lott's House

Portfolio
Suffolk

The heart of East Anglia, Suffolk is bordered by Norfolk, Essex and Cambridgeshire.
As well as Glynn's home, it is a happy hunting ground for any artist with its medieval villages,
Victorian seaside towns, fishing harbours and ancient buildings. All of Glynn's favourite haunts
are here, from the inland beauty spots of Flatford, Kersey, Polstead and Lavenham to the coastal
charm of Aldeburgh, Southwold and Walberswick.

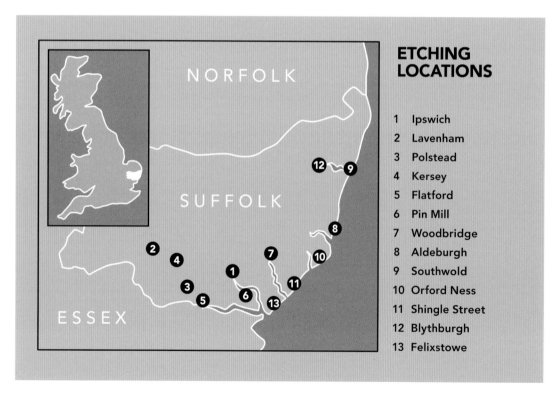

ETCHING LOCATIONS

1 Ipswich
2 Lavenham
3 Polstead
4 Kersey
5 Flatford
6 Pin Mill
7 Woodbridge
8 Aldeburgh
9 Southwold
10 Orford Ness
11 Shingle Street
12 Blythburgh
13 Felixstowe

➤ **Maritime Ipswich**
1999 – 39 x 28 cm

This isn't a scene many visitors to Ipswich will recognise, as it is far removed from the town's rather more modern centre and its familiar high-street shops. But Ipswich was once a significant port, and still has quayside features and can accommodate smaller vessels. The Maritime Ipswich Festival is a very popular event, celebrating all things nautical and bringing together Ipswich's waterfront past and present at the town's docks. As well as the tall-masted sailing ships and many smaller traditional boats, the area is thronged with people in period costume, organising recreational activities for locals and tourists alike. The Ipswich Dock is an area of land at a bend of the River Orwell that has been used for trade since at least the 8th century. A wet dock was constructed in 1842, the biggest enclosed dock in Britain at the time. The early waterfront of Ipswich Dock ran from around St Peter's Church, near the present Stoke Bridge, eastward behind the present quay and past the Custom House.

> ➤ **Lavenham**
> *1986 – 29 x 20 cm*
> ➤➤ **Lavenham**
> *1999 – 39 x 28 cm*

Lavenham is an architectural treasure trove, much loved by tourists and largely unspoilt. It prospered from the wool trade in the 15th and 16th centuries, with the town's blue broadcloth being a notable export. In the medieval period, it was among the 20 wealthiest settlements in England. The Guildhall of the wool guild of Corpus Christi stands in the centre of the village, overlooking the market square, here graced by Morris dancers (near right). Built originally in 1529, most of the timber-framed structure seen today dates from the 17th century and is now maintained by The National Trust. One of Lavenham's worst-kept recent secrets is that scenes from 'Harry Potter and the Deathly Hallows – Parts 1 & 2' were filmed in the market square. From miles away when approaching this small medieval town, the 15th-century church of St Peter and St Paul can be seen casting its imposing shadow on the landscape. In Glynn's 1999 print of Lavenham (far right) the church takes centre stage, emphasising its sheer size that owes much to the cloth-making wealth of the town in its prime. Lavenham's riches helped finance the church with its 141-foot tower – said to be the tallest for a village church in Britain.

➤ Polstead Meadow
1999 – 18 cm diameter

A pretty Suffolk village located across the River Box from Stoke by Nayland, Polstead featured in the Domesday Book. Its name derives from the ponds below a steep hill leading to the village green on one side, with St Mary's church and Polstead Hall on the other. Unusually for a print, Glynn's picture can be heard as well as seen. Inspired by his charming pastoral scene, a local folk group, The Hose Pipe Band, composed and recorded several tunes for a collection named 'Polstead Meadow'.

◄ Kersey Cottages
2000 – 20 x 10 cm

The age and character of Kersey's ancient buildings is captured here, along with the rolling green hills of Suffolk that surround the village. With a population of around 350, the parish of Kersey comprises Kersey village and four hamlets – Kersey Tye, Kersey Upland, Wicker Street Green and William's Green. The village of Kersey, with its famous ford, rises up the slopes of a small valley and is crowned by the church on the south side. One of the most picturesque villages in East Anglia, Kersey boasts an important collection of medieval buildings, such as those seen here in Glynn's picture. First mentioned in an Anglo-Saxon will of about AD900, Kersey was already a thriving community at the time of the Norman Conquest in 1066. The Domesday Book mentions a church 'with three acres'. Sheep rearing figured prominently in the pattern of farming recorded in the Domesday Book, and many believe that the village derived considerable wealth from the wool trade, like other local towns such as Hadleigh and Lavenham.

∧ Flatford

2012 – 33 cm diameter

Thanks to landscape painter John Constable, Flatford is one of East Anglia's most familiar locations, but even the great Constable couldn't put Glynn's unmistakable spin on the cluster of ancient buildings and waterways. The heart of the hamlet is Flatford Mill, built in 1733. This imposing Grade I-listed red-brick building features in a number of Constable paintings. The National Trust acquired the mill in 1943, and it is now leased to the Field Studies Council. Across the millstream is Willy Lott's House, seen in Constable's 'The Hay Wain'. The original name, Gibbonsgate Farm, was changed after its Constable appearance.

Valley Farm is the oldest building at Flatford. Built in the mid-15th century, it is a medieval great hall house that was home to wealthy yeoman farmers until the early 1900s. Grade I listed, it was renovated in 1938 by private owners, and restored to near original condition following the National Trust's acquisition in 1959.

Glynn Thomas

◄ Footpath to Dedham
2012 – 29 x 20 cm

The walk from Flatford to Dedham (and
back) attracts millions who wish to walk
in Constable's footsteps. Glynn here
shows the way using the public footpath
and the river bank, via Fen Bridge and
Dedham Bridge, through water meadows
and cattle pasture to the well-preserved
Essex village.

∧ Flatford Bridge
2012 – 19 x 33 cm

The beautiful walk alongside the River
Stour from Dedham village to Flatford
delivers you here, within easy reach of
the welcoming tea room and just a bun's
throw from hungry ducks, geese and
swans. The wooden bridge, rebuilt many
times over the centuries, is normally too
thick with tourists to appreciate. It and the
thatched Bridge Cottage (which houses
the Constable museum) may have been
painted by the great man, but never
quite like this!

➤ Pin Mill

1999 – 62 x 19 cm

A great spot for boat enthusiasts through
the ages, the small community of Pin
Mill lies at the water's edge, providing
a perfect vantage point from which to
watch the annual Pin Mill Barge Match,
which brings together restored sailing
barges every July. Glynn's picture not only
illustrates some of these mighty trading
vessels but showcases the other main Pin
Mill attraction – the Butt & Oyster public
house. Often found frequenting the bar
are those few remaining workmen with
the skills to repair the barges and other
traditional boats. The pub is reputed to
have been a secret rendezvous for the
Duke and Duchess of Windsor when he
was Prince of Wales and she was Mrs
Simpson, awaiting her decree nisi in
nearby Felixstowe.

➤ Woodbridge Tide Mill
2003 – 62 x 19 cm

The earliest record of a tide mill operating on this site by the River Deben is from 1170. Owned by the Augustinian Priors for around 350 years, the original Woodbridge Tide Mill was confiscated by King Henry VIII in 1536 and was in royal ownership for 28 years before Queen Elizabeth I sold it to Thomas Seckford in 1564. His family then owned it for more than 100 years, before a succession of other private owners. In 1793, the present mill was built on the site, and by the 1950s it was the last working tide mill in the country. It closed in 1957, but was salvaged in 1968 and opened to the public in 1973. Recent restoration work has brought it back into use as a fully working tide mill. Now, when tides permit, the five-metre, four-tonne English oak waterwheel turns the machinery, and grain is milled to produce flour. As well as installing a replacement water wheel, which was made by the International Boatbuilding Training College in Lowestoft, the restoration has included improvements to the foundations to stop the mill slipping into the Deben.

⌃ Aldeburgh Beach
2006 – 28 x 72 cm

The name Aldeburgh used to be split into two words, Alde and Burgh. Alde Burgh literally means 'old fort', and there was once a fortification on the site. However, this was lost to the sea along with much of the original Tudor town. Aldeburgh once had a flourishing shipping and shipbuilding industry (and still has a modest fishing fleet), but the town went into decline when the River Alde became silted and was unable to accommodate larger ships. Aldeburgh then survived largely as a fishing village until the 19th century, when tourism took over as the main business. Here Glynn shows the shingle beach and many of Aldeburgh's key attractions. Having failed to persuade a fishing boat to take him out to get a sailor's-eye view, he took to his canoe for a risky excursion that drenched his notebook but resulted in one of his most popular prints. Kites make one of many appearances in his seaside scenes, along with gulls and fishing boats. The lifeboat station and Aldeburgh Beach South Lookout are prominent features.

As in many of Glynn's seaside scenes, the Great British Public is immortalised. On Aldeburgh Beach, all age groups and body shapes can be spotted having a paddle.

Queueing for fish and chips is another Aldeburgh speciality, but most people think they're worth the wait. Here, holidaymakers sit on the wall and keep up the tradition.

Look closely and you can make out Iken Church and Snape Maltings, located just a few miles inland on the River Alde. Typical with Glynn's work, you get three places in one!

Old Custom House Aldeburgh
2006 – 14 x 13 cm

Cats are regular visitors to Glynn Thomas locations, and the one here is waiting at the unusual raised front door of the Old Custom House in Aldeburgh. Unlike the neighbouring properties, the c.1703 building has a flight of eight stone-faced brick steps up to the six-panel door. The big 20-panel ground-floor windows are situated much lower down – and rather over-sized in comparison. These, apparently, were a later addition, and one has since been converted to a glazed door. Adjoining the Old Custom House are Rosemary Cottage and Lavender Cottage, built around 1600 and once forming a single Suffolk timber-framed house. In the background of Glynn's picture can be seen the famous Napoleonic-era Martello tower to the south.

◀ **Aldeburgh Boats**
2011 – 14 X 10 cm

The days of big ships at Aldeburgh are long gone, but fishing boats are still dragged up on to the shingle beach to unload their catch, with fishermen selling their daily haul to locals, visitors and Aldeburgh restaurants. The town's most famous fisherman is probably Peter Grimes, subject of a Benjamin Britten opera, while the prosaically named but greatly lauded Aldeburgh Fish & Chip Shop on the high street sees long queues every day throughout the season. The gulls featuring in Glynn's fishing boat scene will gladly help tourists finish their lunch.

▼ **Aldeburgh Rooftops**
2000 – 13 x 42 cm

At the top of the Town Steps, leading off the High Street and up the cliff, there is a wonderful view over the rooftops and out to sea. Since the River Alde silted up and prevented bigger ships and boats gaining access, Aldeburgh survived principally as a fishing village until the 19th century, when it became popular as a seaside resort. Much of its distinctive and whimsical architecture derives from this period. The river is now home to a yacht club and a sailing club. There is an account of the town's setting and beginning as a holiday resort in the fourth scene of Wilkie Collins' 1862 novel 'No Name'.

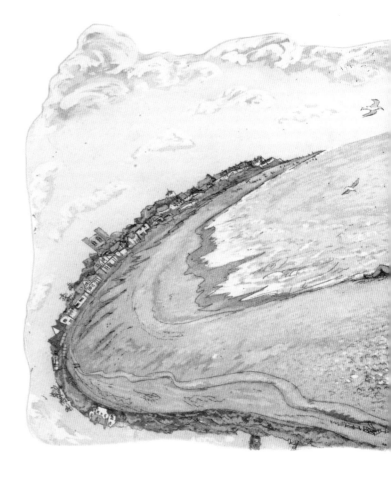

◄ Moot Hall

2011 – 37 x 13 cm

For more than 400 years, Aldeburgh town councillors have been meeting at the Grade I-listed Moot Hall, which still houses the town clerk's office as well as the local museum. The timber-framed hall was built around 1520 and altered in 1654. The brick and stone infilling of the ground floor took place much later, but helps give the building its unusual appearance. Moot Hall was restored and the external staircase and gable ends rebuilt in 1854–5 under the direction of R M Phipson, the chief architect of the Diocese of Norwich. Phipson was responsible for many important church renovations in Suffolk, and got the Moot Hall job because Aldeburgh at that time came under the Bishop of Norwich. Beyond Glynn's depiction of the ancient building are Aldeburgh's familiar fishing boats and the huts selling the catch straight from the sea.

∧ Britten's Beach
2011 – 13 x 42 cm

Maggi Hambling's public sculpture 'The Scallop' on the beach at Aldeburgh has aroused strong feelings since it was unveiled in November 2003. Dedicated to composer Benjamin Britten, who became a resident of the town in 1942, the artwork was created from stainless steel by Suffolk-born and based Hambling. Standing four metres high, the piece is made up of two interlocking scallop shells, each broken, the upright shell being pierced with the words: 'I hear those voices that will not be drowned', taken from Britten's opera 'Peter Grimes'. Approached along the road from the Thorpeness direction, the sculpture has a very different silhouette, resembling a knight on a rearing charger. Opinion is divided between those who believe that such a beautiful natural setting should not have been 'spoilt' by the addition of a large, man-made structure, and those who feel that The Scallop fits in well with the landscape. If you agree with the critics, Glynn's striking print may not be for you!

◄ Adnams
1993 – 14 x 3 cm

George and Ernest Adnams in 1872 bought the Sole Bay Brewery in Southwold with the help of their father. A few years later George was eaten by a crocodile in South Africa, so clearly should have stuck with supplying beer to Suffolk's pubs and hotels. Situated under the Southwold lighthouse, the Sole Bay Inn was built in around 1835 and is the closest pub to the brewery, as well as being just two minutes from the sea.

➤ Southwold
1986 – 27 x 40 cm

In 1659, a fire destroyed much of Southwold, resulting in large-scale re-planning and rebuilding. This led to the creation of a series of distinctive Southwold 'greens' designed to act as fire breaks in the event of another disaster. The clusters of housing are therefore kept separate by these recreational areas, each complete with benches for the use of weary locals and visitors alike. Beneath these greens it is believed that some of the ruins of the properties destroyed in the fire may still be found – although amateur excavations are not encouraged!

∨ Free Lunch
2003 – 8 x 22 cm

For most visitors to Southwold Harbour, lunch can readily be found in the form of fish and chips, or fresh seafood straight off the small fleet of boats. Here, Glynn catches some of the harbour's many gulls when helping themselves as boats ply the narrow stretch of water separating Southwold from Walberswick. The pedestrian-only ferry can be seen carrying tourists across, saving a 30-minute round trip by car. The meeting here of the River Blyth and the North Sea means sailors need considerable skill to bring their boats into or out of the harbour.

▾ The Nelson
1997 – 6 x 9 cm

The Nelson was originally the Noah's Ark, possibly built in 1672 during the reign of King Charles II. It retained this name until some time between 1790 and 1805, but then became the Lord Nelson as Britain's greatest seaman captured the public imagination.

▾ Harbour Inn, Southwold
1997 – 6 x 9 cm

The Harbour Inn is arguably too close to the sea, as it is one of the most frequently flooded pubs in Suffolk. Located on the River Blyth at Southwold Harbour, it has a sign on its front wall showing the level of the 1953 great flood. Rising water from the tidal estuary still causes problems.

∧ Lighthouse Southwold
2007 – 13 x 42 cm

Neither on a cliff edge nor on a rocky island offshore, Southwold lighthouse sits incongruously among the houses behind the promenade. The white-painted tower was built in 1887 by national lighthouse operator Trinity House as a replacement for three local lighthouses that were under serious threat from coastal erosion. It began operation in 1890 and was electrified and de-manned in 1938. The lighthouse is unusual in that the light itself is switched on and off in sequence (four flashes every 20 seconds) rather than using lenses to create a rotating beam. It is possible to climb up the tower during the tourist season, through arrangement with Trinity House. Glynn's lighthouse-eye view of Southwold town and seafront shows the 1946-built steamer 'Waverley' heading for the pier – a familiar scene just a few years ago.

▼ The Ferryman
1997 – 8 x 45 cm

Walberswick boasts one of Britain's smallest regular ferry services. Glynn shows the rowing boat with a full complement making its way between Southwold Harbour and Walberswick across the River Blyth. The print features the late David Church, the ferryman for many years before his daughter Dani took up the oars. When crossing the river, the strength of the tide has to be taken into account, so rowing has to be into the flow of water. The ferry welcomes dogs and bicycles, but if you arrive by car you'll have to look elsewhere for a lift!

46

▲ Southwold Summer
2003 – 28 x 62 cm

In spite of the great fire of 1659 that destroyed much of the original seaside town, Southwold still contains many buildings of historic and architectural interest. Glynn's panoramic view includes the impressive Church of St Edmund, which was built in the late 15th century; and, of course, the unmistakable Trinity House lighthouse. Also depicted are the many shops that march up and down the High Street; the Southwold Museum, housed in its post-fire premises; the Electric Picture Palace cinema; the marketplace with its town pump and jubilee clock; and the Adnams Brewery site. Until recently, the heavy horse and dray cart shown in Glynn's picture still hauled barrels of beer around the town. To the top right of the image is Gun Hill, where six cannons are sited, pointing out to sea.

Southwold Pier
2010 – 19 x 33 cm

While Southwold has had a pier since 1900, the one currently enjoyed by visitors and locals is a much more recent construction. In fact, it is Britain's first and only 21st-century pier, completed in 2001. The original version was built as a landing stage for passenger steamships that cruised along the east coast from London Bridge. The restored Clyde-built paddle steamer 'Waverley' was until relatively recently a visitor to the pier. In 1934, the T-shaped landing stage was swept away in a violent storm and never replaced. At the outbreak of WWII, the pier was sectioned for fear of use in a German invasion. A drifting sea mine then caused further damage in 1941, before much of the pier was washed away in 1955. Private buyers took charge of the remains in 1987, beginning a rebuilding programme in 1999. Southwold Pier now extends 623 feet into the sea.

Glynn Thomas

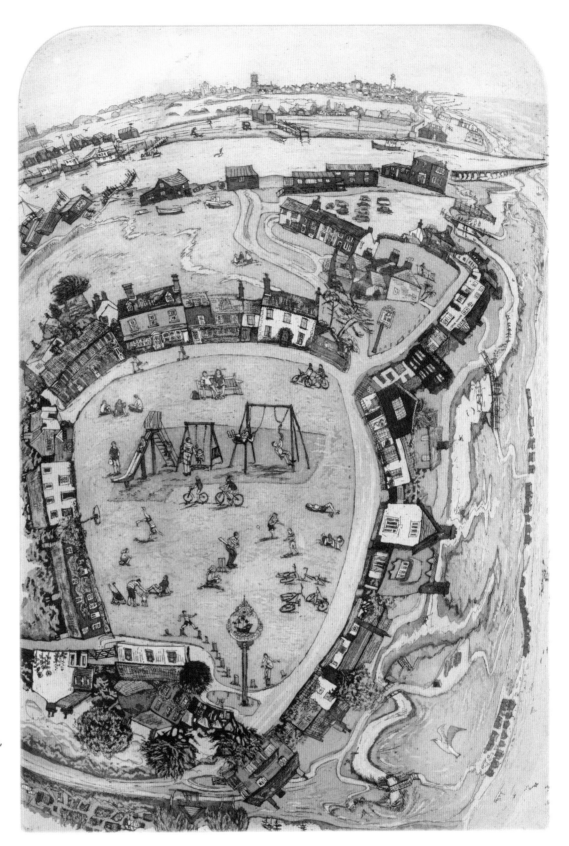

› Walberswick Green
2011 – 39 x 28 cm

The name Walberswick is believed to derive from the Saxon 'Waldbert' – probably a landowner – and 'wyc', meaning shelter or harbour. At the top of the village is the 15th-century St Andrew's Church, which appears over-sized in relation to the village, but reflects its once important role as a thriving port trading in cheese, bacon, corn, timber and fish from the 13th century until the First World War. With more than 1,000 acres of heath and marshland protected within the Suffolk Coast and Heaths Area of Outstanding Natural Beauty, Walberswick provides a varied habitat for birds, but also attracts craftsmen and artists. In the 1890s and early 1900s, the village became associated with Philip Wilson Steer and his circle of 'English Impressionist' painters. It was also home to artist and architect Charles Rennie Mackintosh from 1914. Visible in Glynn's print, the ornate metalwork sign to the village was erected in 1953 in commemoration of the coronation of Queen Elizabeth II. As well as the slide and swings on the Green, a major attraction for children in summer is crabbing by the harbour, where bridges and river banks become crammed with buckets and fishing lines.

‹ Southwold Beach Huts
1998 – 26 x 44 cm

Southwold has a permanent population of just over 1,500 and comprises approximately 1,250 residential properties, of which more than a third are either second homes or holiday lets. In addition, there are around 300 beach huts that thread their way along the shoreline from Gun Hill to the pier and beyond. These highly desirable but rather fragile buildings evolved from fishermen's shacks and bathing huts. Most are occupied (though not after nightfall) only during the holiday season, but some hardy types use theirs almost daily. The huts can change hands for the price of a very smart car or a very small house, so Glynn's print is perhaps the most economical way of enjoying the experience.

Lighthouse Orfordness
2008 – 26 x 44 cm

Orford Ness contains some 15 per cent of the world's reserve of coastal vegetated shingle, and is Europe's biggest shingle spit of its kind. Just walking on the fragile terrain can cause lasting damage. Now owned by the National Trust, it is perhaps the organisation's least likely 'beauty spot', as it is littered with the decaying remains of a military history. For most of the 20th century the island was used for secret experiments on a vast range of lethal weapons. It was used intensively as a bombing and rocket range, with the result that potentially dangerous debris remains. Glynn's picture focuses on the William Watkins-designed Orfordness Lighthouse, but also shows the radio transmitting station and the strange pagoda-like structures built for atomic bomb testing. The powerful medium-wave radio station was owned originally by the Foreign Office, then the BBC, and is best known for transmitting the BBC World Service in English from September 1982 until March 2011. The lighthouse tower dates from 1792, and in 1836 Trinity House bought it from the third Lord Braybrooke for £13,414. In 1959, the lighthouse was converted to electric power; and on 6 July 1964 became fully automatic.

⋀ Shingle Street
1986 – 6 x 9 cm

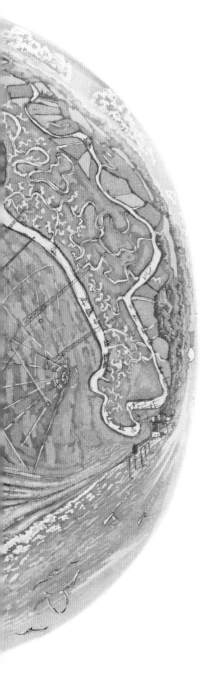

Located on the Suffolk Heritage Coast, just a few miles north of Felixstowe, this single row of buildings faces the North Sea just feet away across shifting banks of shingle. There is a dead-end road from Hollesley, a couple of miles inland, that runs behind the houses. A rough footpath runs along the front and there are virtually no visitor facilities, except for car parking. The first habitation of Shingle Street appears to have been in the early 1800s, when the Martello towers were built. Fisherman then threw up rough shacks and primitive cottages and acted as pilots when the mouth of the River Ore was just to the south of Shingle Street. The Martello tower at Shingle Street is known as 'AA'. Once the initial function (as a deterrent for French invaders) became redundant, the tower was used to house coastguards. In 1940, the inhabitants of Shingle Street were evacuated so that the beach could be mined against invasion. The army took over the houses and, later, the Royal Air Force used the buildings for experimental bombing. Among the surviving buildings are the Coastguard Cottages, The Mansion, Kate's Cottage and Windy Ridge, plus the Martello tower. A report in 2004 suggested that, unless the sea defences in the area were strengthened, Shingle Street could disappear within 20 years.

⋀ Blythburgh Church
1997 – 8 x 7 cm

Blythburgh village stands within an Area of Outstanding Natural Beauty just four miles inland from Southwold on Suffolk's Heritage Coast. While the village is bisected by the busy A12, the dominant feature is Holy Trinity, acclaimed as one of the county's finest medieval churches. Standing on high ground overlooking the fields and marshland of the Blyth Valley, the church forms a memorable landmark that is floodlit at night to spectacular effect. Rebuilt in around 1480, the church originally had extensive and elaborate stained-glass windows, but most didn't survive the Protestant ascendancy in the 16th century. By the late 17th century the church was in a very sad state, and it took a national campaign in the 1880s to repair and reopen Holy Trinity.

➤ Getting Shipshape
2003 – 15 x 23 cm

There may not be many commercial fishing boats left at Southwold Harbour, but they still have a job to do and need to be kept in good order if they are to bring back the daily catch to the numerous fresh fish huts along the Blyth. Among the boats currently found in the river are vessels built in Felixstowe, Aldeburgh, Woodbridge, Southwold and Walberswick. Almost all are of clinker construction, mostly larch on oak, and generally around 18 feet in length.

Felixstowe Ferry
2003 – 13 x 42 cm

Located just two miles to the north east of Felixstowe, with its major container port, this charming hamlet is a great place for fresh fish, caught locally and sold from huts on the quayside. There is indeed a ferry, transporting people across the mouth of the River Deben to the Bawdsey peninsula. Tucked away to the far right of Glynn's picture are the two Napoleonic Martello towers that dominate the seafront. St Nicholas's Church was once a major feature of the small village, built in 1954 on the site of an earlier church destroyed by German bombing in 1943. However, very little of it remains.

Sole Bay
1997 – 20 x 10 cm

Suffolk's Sole Bay is today known best for its fishing boats and fresh fish sellers, rather than for the fierce naval engagement of 1672 between English and French fleets on one side and the Dutch (under Michiel de Ruyter) on the other. The Battle of Sole Bay, off Southwold, was bloody but indecisive, and many bodies were washed ashore on the town's beaches. Southwold Museum has a collection of mementos of the event. In those distant days, Southwold provided plenty of entertainment for sailors, thanks to several ale houses, and many of the crew and marines were enjoying shore leave when the Dutch fleet sailed into view. Glynn's depiction of a jetty, boats, nets and crab pots is a rather more familiar scene for today's visitors.

Essex

Linking East Anglia with London, Essex is densely populated and highly urbanised to the west, while boasting popular seaside resorts to the east. Glynn's eye is drawn particularly to the many appealing waterside locations such as Maldon, Wivenhoe, Leigh-on-Sea, Heybridge, Mistley, Walton-on-the-Naze and Mersea Island.

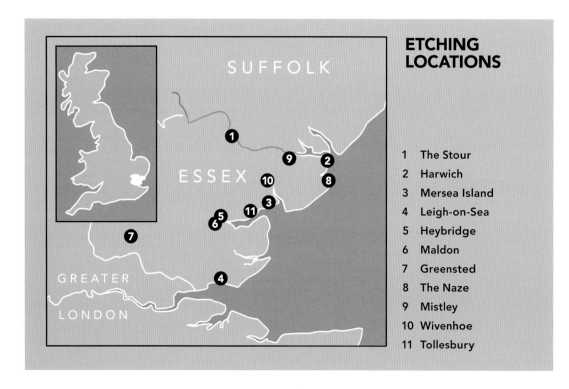

ETCHING LOCATIONS

1 The Stour
2 Harwich
3 Mersea Island
4 Leigh-on-Sea
5 Heybridge
6 Maldon
7 Greensted
8 The Naze
9 Mistley
10 Wivenhoe
11 Tollesbury

➤ **Along the Stour**
1979 – 48 x 34 cm

This tranquil scene, with its yellow 'brandy bottle' pond lilies, is of the River Stour running through Essex and into Suffolk. The 47-mile waterway forms most of the county boundary between Suffolk to the north and Essex to the south. It rises in eastern Cambridgeshire, passes to the east of Haverhill, through Cavendish, Sudbury, Stratford St Mary and Dedham, and flows through the Dedham Vale Area of Outstanding Natural Beauty. The river becomes tidal just after Manningtree in Essex, and joins the North Sea at Harwich. The eastern part of the River Stour is an Area of Outstanding Natural Beauty known as Dedham Vale, named after the village of Dedham in Essex. Glynn's print was commissioned by Christie's Contemporary Art in 1979.

56

◄ Harwich
1983 – 26 x 40 cm

Harwich is a busy coastal town and international freight/ferry port located on the estuary of the rivers Stour and Orwell in north-east Essex. The old town of Harwich is a conservation area containing many historic buildings. An impressive 180-foot diameter circular fort was built in 1808 to defend the port against a Napoleonic invasion. It is the only such example open to the public. Eleven guns are sited on the battlements. Part of the fort is now used as a military museum. There are interesting nautical displays housed in the town's decommissioned lighthouse, which provides great views over the harbour and its relentless shipping movements. The lighthouse that previously occupied this site was painted by John Constable, possibly around 1800. The present lighthouse was built, along with the high lighthouse a few hundred yards away, in 1818.

▲ Ha'penny Pier Harwich
1993 – 8 x 22 cm

As depicted here by Glynn, the Pier Ticket Office is a charming, typical example of late 19th-century architecture. It once had two storeys, but was built without the bell cage. The ticket office now houses the Ha'penny Pier Visitor Centre, as well as the 'Christopher Jones and the Mayflower' exhibition. Work began on this pier in 1852 and it was opened in July 1853. It took its name from the halfpenny toll charged. Originally the pier was twice as long as the present one, but one half burnt down in 1927. It was a popular departure point for paddle steamers until after the First World War. The area of water enclosed by the arm of the pier is known as the Pound. Berthed here is a remnant of the once great 19th-century fishing fleet. The pier also accommodates the lifeboat house for the RNLI inshore rescue boat.

Glynn Thomas

◀ Mersea Island
1989 – 19 x 33 cm

Located around eight miles from Colchester in Essex, Mersea Island is situated between the estuaries of the Colne and Blackwater rivers. This is the most easterly inhabited island in the British Isles and is separated into West Mersea and East Mersea, with both areas having individual attributes. West Mersea is the main area with the largest population, and East Mersea is the more rural. The Strood is the 1,000 metre-long causeway that connects Mersea with the 'mainland'. Built originally by the Saxons, it gets covered by the tide a few times each month, trapping the unwary. The main activities on Mersea are farming, fishing (including oyster gathering) and servicing the leisure boat industry. In WWII, 2,000 troops were stationed on the island to guard against invasion. Two batteries of 4.7-inch guns were installed and, while the one at East Mersea was demolished, the battery at West Mersea became a café.

▼ Leigh-on-Sea
1991 – 13 x 42 cm

On the north bank of the River Thames, around 30 miles east of London and in the borough of Southend-on-Sea, stands the old fishing village of Leigh-on-Sea, mentioned in the Domesday Book as Legra. With increasing seaborne trade during the Middle Ages, the settlement exploited its sheltered position on the important shipping route to London and grew quickly. By the 13th century it had its own parish church, St Clements, although the current building in the town dates from the 15th century. By the 16th century Leigh had become a fairly large and prosperous port, handling coastal and Continental trade, especially with France and Holland. Shipbuilding became a major activity, and 'The Mayflower', the 100-foot three-masted ship in which the Pilgrim Fathers made their 1620 voyage to America, was either built or owned in Leigh. During the 18th century, sailing ships became larger and the sea

level rose, resulting in the silting up of Leigh's deepwater channel. As a result, the town went into rapid decline, and reverted quickly to a fishing village. It was the arrival of the London, Tilbury and Southend railway line in 1854 that revived Leigh's fortunes, with the fishing industry quick to take advantage of this new and speedy form of transport. South of the railway track lies Leigh Old Town, packed with old-world charm and character. As depicted by Glynn, historic buildings are scattered along the High Street, including the Old Smithy, rebuilt from two earlier cottages in 1860–1880 and now containing a Heritage Centre. The Leigh Conservation Area to the north of the railway line rises from the Old Town up the steep hillside to the parish church at the top. This area contains large numbers of attractive, old terraced houses and cottages with ancient architectural features.

◄ Heybridge Basin Low Tide
2010 – 19 x 33 cm

Mud, boats and lock gates grab the eye in this etching, which shows the Heybridge Basin at low tide. It forms the start of the Chelmer & Blackwater Navigation, and it was here that the colliers' barges unloaded for the journey inland. Construction of the 13-mile canal to Chelmsford began in 1793 under the general direction of John Rennie. The basin at Heybridge was dug out at the sea end of the navigation to allow lighters to enter the canal via the sea lock for the unloading of their cargoes for transportation inland. The stretch of canal between the Basin and Beeleigh was cut out by hand to bypass Maldon because the town opposed the building of the canal, fearing loss of trade in the port. Today, Heybridge Basin is a haven for pleasure craft of all ages and sizes, as well as being the starting point for walks along the sea wall to Maldon. There is an annual Heybridge Basin regatta, usually held in early July.

▲ Heybridge Boats
2010 – 6 x 14 cm

With the fragile jetties, mud left by the departing tide and the restored Thames sailing barge, this evocative Essex coastal scene captures Heybridge, near Maldon. The name Heybridge came from the high bridge that was built over the River Blackwater in the Middle Ages. Some people believe that the Blackwater at Heybridge, near where the bridge was later built, was the site of the Battle of Maldon. The Heybridge Basin is located where the Chelmer & Blackwater Navigation Canal merges into the tidal Blackwater Estuary, fed by the rivers Blackwater and Chelmer. The two rivers are linked by a lock that is used regularly by pleasure boats.

⌃ Maldon Hythe

2010 – 18 x 58 cm

The Hythe, as the port at Maldon is
known, began life as a separate hamlet.
The skyline is dominated by the tower
of St Mary's Church, shown to the left
of centre in Glynn's picture. In the past,
Thames barges (in the foreground) would
leave the Hythe carrying foodstuffs and
bedding straw to London, returning with
cargoes of horse manure for the district
farms. Fishing vessels left their moorings
by the bath wall in search of eels, plaice,
sole, whelks and winkles in the estuary.
Some of the old fishermen's homes remain,
and can be seen in a row facing the quay.

> Greensted Church
1991 – 6 x 9 cm

Possibly the most ancient building to be reproduced by Glynn in this book, St Andrew's, Greensted, is believed to be the oldest wooden church in the world. Representing some 1,300 years of English history, it is also the oldest 'stave-built' timber building in Europe, with the 51 timber planks dating back to 1060 – before King Harold lost his life to William the Conqueror. Excavations undertaken during 1960 in the chancel revealed the existence of two earlier timber structures dating from the 6th and 7th centuries. The church shows evidence of the work of Saxon, Norman, Tudor and Victorian builders, who repaired, restored and extended the building during its epic lifespan. The body of Saint Edmund, King of East Anglia, and England's first patron saint martyred in 869AD, rested in the church in 1013 on its way to Bury St. Edmunds in Suffolk. In 1990, works were carried out to stabilise the building; and in 2005, the spire was completely re-shingled in oak. The oldest grave in the churchyard, lying adjacent to the entrance of the church, is that of a 12th-century Crusader, thought to be a bowman.

⌃ Naze Tower

2009 – 26 cm diameter

The Naze Tower is an historic 86ft landmark situated on an attractive stretch of coastline at Walton-on-the-Naze in Essex. Over eight floors, it houses an art gallery, a museum, tearooms and a roof platform with panoramic views – although none quite as spectacular as those in Glynn's print. The Naze cliffs are designated a Site of Special Scientific Interest due to their geology, which makes them popular with fossil hunters. The tower itself was built in 1721 by Trinity House long before lighthouses became commonplace. Its original purpose was to act as a marker for ships approaching Harwich Harbour. At the beginning of the 20th century radio masts were erected at the top in an attempt at long-range transmission. If coastal erosion continues uninterrupted, the tower could be lost to the sea, much like the cliffs below it.

> ### Mistley Quay
> *2011 – 29 x 20 cm*

Glynn's depiction of Mistley Quay will sadden and gladden in equal measure. It shows the delightful Essex waterside location before it became a 'prisoner' of the quay owners in September 2008, fenced off and ending 500 years of free access to the water. Not only were parents and children no longer able to feed the 250-plus swans, but the wonderful panoramic view of the River Stour was disrupted. Birdwatchers, attracted by large numbers of waders and migratory species, are also victims of the unwelcome enclosure. A portion of sales proceeds from Glynn's Mistley Quay print go to the 'Free the Quay' campaign. The first part of the quay in Mistley, which is in the Tendring district of north-east Essex, around 11 miles from Colchester and adjoining Manningtree, was built around 1725. There was onward trading to Manningtree, and by horse-drawn and poled lighters through the upper reaches to Sudbury. Some 50 years later the quay was enlarged and became the Port of Mistley. As this book went to press, there were signs that the local council might bring the fence affair to a satisfactory conclusion, and that Mistley Quay might be set free.

66

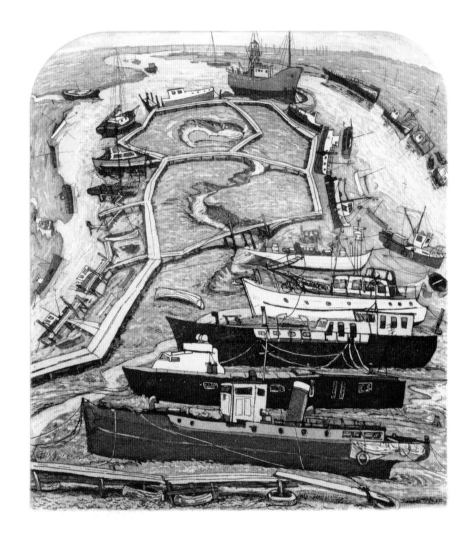

◄ Wivenhoe Quay
1991 – 26 x 40 cm

Wivenhoe's long and colourful history involves oysters, fishing, sailing boats, trading ships and smuggling. The current church, seen to the right of Glynn's print with a distinctive cupola atop its sturdy tower, inhabits the site of a much earlier version, built in Saxon times. Artists and craftsmen have long been attracted to the small Essex town, located just three miles from Colchester but worlds apart in terms of the pace of life. The streets are small and quaint, many with great architectural interest, as can be seen from the picture. Most lead ultimately to the picturesque waterfront where fishing boats and sailing craft are moored. Wivenhoe Quay was once effectively the port for nearby Colchester, as trading vessels could get no farther up the River Colne. Much of lower Wivenhoe is a designated conservation area.

▲ Tollesbury Saltings
1991 – 20 x 18 cm

Boats, ships and the snaking timber staging that provides access to them are the dominant features of Glynn's print depicting the Saltings at the Essex village of Tollesbury, on the mouth of the River Blackwater, nine miles east of Maldon. The village sits on a small peninsula, with Tollesbury Fleet and Old Hall marshes to the north, and the River Blackwater to the south. Its location makes the village popular with bird spotters, walkers and sailors. Tollesbury has for centuries relied on harvests from both land and sea, so the village has become known as 'The Village of the Plough and Sail'. The well-maintained network of footpaths and boardwalks allows sailors access to the berths at the Saltings. Water access to the creek is dependent on the tide and the depth of the vessel. Tollesbury Saltings enjoys between one and two hours either side of high tide.

Cambridgeshire

Dominated by the university city of Cambridge, with historic colleges, courts and churches, the county is also Glynn's birthplace and holds fond memories. While his work has dwelled upon the architectural splendour of the university landscape, he has roamed farther afield to capture the majesty of Ely and the old-world charm of St Ives.

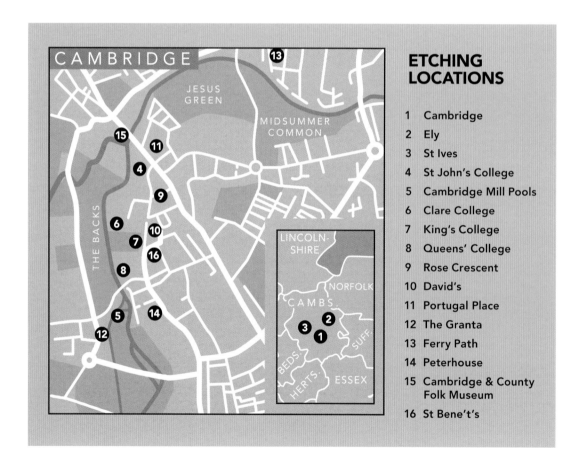

ETCHING LOCATIONS

1 Cambridge
2 Ely
3 St Ives
4 St John's College
5 Cambridge Mill Pools
6 Clare College
7 King's College
8 Queens' College
9 Rose Crescent
10 David's
11 Portugal Place
12 The Granta
13 Ferry Path
14 Peterhouse
15 Cambridge & County Folk Museum
16 St Bene't's

➤ **Cambridge Courts**
1993 – 64 x 41 cm

This panoramic view captures some of the great colleges and their courts, with St John's, Trinity, King's and Queens' all visible in Glynn's etching. The River Cam and The Backs take up the right-hand side of the picture. The famous Round Church, or Church of the Holy Sepulchre, appears in the foreground. Trinity Great Court, completed in the early years of the 17th century, is reputed to be the largest enclosed court in Europe. Second Court at St John's, built from 1598 to 1602, has been described as the finest Tudor court in England. St John's New Court, or 'The Wedding Cake', is probably one of the best-known buildings in Cambridge. Much of the Old Court at Queens' College was erected in 1448, possibly designed by the master mason Reginald Ely, who built the original Old Court of King's College at the same time.

∧ Cambridge
1997 – 64 x 41 cm

The city of Cambridge rivals Oxford as the ultimate university town, swamped with elegant and important architecture, awash with gifted students and submerged under a sea of summer tourists. There is archaeological evidence of a Bronze Age settlement in the area; and under Viking rule Cambridge became an important trading centre. The first town charters were granted in the 12th century. It is the University of Cambridge, founded in 1209, that

defines the city, and Glynn's panoramic view takes in most of the key colleges. Cambridge is ranked consistently as one of the top five universities in the world. The skyline is dominated by King's College Chapel and the Cambridge University Library. The green space of Parker's Piece hosted the very first game of association football, and the famed Strawberry Fair music and arts festival is held on Midsummer Common. After the Romans left the area, the Saxons took

over the land on and around Castle Hill and renamed it Grantabrycge – 'Bridge over the River Granta'. Over time, the name evolved to become Cambridge, while the River Granta became known eventually as the River Cam. In 1068, two years after his conquest of England, William of Normandy built a castle on Castle Hill, and the town fell under the control of the king and his deputies. The City's distinctive Round Church dates from this period. In 1209, Cambridge

University was founded by students escaping from hostile townspeople in Oxford. The oldest existing college, Peterhouse, was founded in 1284. One of the best-known buildings, King's College Chapel, was begun in 1446 by King Henry VI, and completed in 1515 during the reign of King Henry VIII. Cambridge was granted its city charter in 1951 in recognition of its history, administrative importance and economic success – it does not have a cathedral, traditionally a prerequisite for city status. The city gained its second university in 1992 when Anglia Polytechnic became Anglia Polytechnic University. Renamed Anglia Ruskin University in 2005, the institution has its origins in Glynn's alma mater, the Cambridge School of Art. The latest honour to be bestowed on the city came on 29 April 2011, when the title The Duke of Cambridge was conferred by The Queen on Prince William following his marriage to Catherine Middleton.

◄ St John's
1999 – 42 x 9 cm

Here Glynn depicts the magnificent St John's College and the view to the so-called 'Wedding Cake' building that is the 19th-century neo-gothic New Court. Alumni of St John's include nine Nobel Prize winners, six prime ministers, three archbishops, at least two princes and three saints. The college was founded in 1511 by Lady Margaret Beaufort, mother of King Henry VII. It is one of the oldest and largest in Cambridge. Originally a seminary focused chiefly on the liberal arts, theology and the biblical languages, St John's became a centre for training of the mind in classics and mathematics. In the 20th century, it developed a strong reputation in medicine and the experimental sciences. The college's distinctive Great Gate is adorned with the arms of Lady Beaufort. Above these are displayed her ensigns, the Red Rose of Lancaster and Portcullis. The College Arms are flanked by mythical beasts known as 'yales'. First Court is entered via the Great Gate, and was converted between 1511 and 1520. Second Court, built from 1598 to 1602, has been described as the finest Tudor court in England. New Court, or The Wedding Cake, is probably one of the best-known buildings in Cambridge, and the first to be built by any of the colleges on the west side of the river.

◄ Rose Crescent
1998 – 42 x 9 cm

Rose Crescent is a popular and attractive pedestrian route into the market, shown at the top of Glynn's picture, and dates largely from the early 19th century. The route follows the approaches and yards to the old Rose Tavern, of which nothing remains. The north-east side of the crescent was laid out as a planned development in 1825, and the south-west side was acquired by Gonville & Caius College, which demolished the old buildings to erect St Michael's Court in 1901–3.

➤ David's
2005 – 42 x 9 cm

Keen readers will enjoy this one. Maybe the shop will even stock this book once it's out of print! Classic Cambridge elements such as the bicycle with basket provide visual clues to the location, even if you miss the punts in the background on the Cam. St Edward's Passage runs between the Guildhall and King's College. David's Bookshop is situated on the northern side of the church, towards the Market Square.

▼ Portugal Place
1997 – 20 x 10 cm

Portugal Place leads north-eastwards from the main Roman and medieval route through this part of Cambridge. In its earliest form, this was a lane along the side of St Clement's Churchyard, believed by some to pre-date the Norman Conquest. Most of the street is much later in date, with gradual extension northwards in the 17th, 18th and 19th centuries. Portugal Place is a narrow, picturesque street and is an attractive antidote to the adjoining shopping routes. The cat that appears in Glynn's work presumably enjoys the peace and tranquility of the lane that leads pedestrians and cyclists to Jesus Green.

The Granta
2010 – 37 x 13 cm

The Granta is punters' paradise – a beautiful riverside location within easy walking distance of Cambridge centre with its own punt station. Visitors by road or river can enjoy the willow-fringed millpond on the banks of the River Cam while supping their pints or sipping Pimms on the riverside patio of the famous public house that neighbours Grantchester Mill. The Granta is also the early name for the Cam, given by the Saxons when the town was known as Grantabrycge – 'Bridge over the River Granta'.

◀ X II III Time IV Tea
2010 – 29 x 20 cm

'Stands the church clock at ten-to-three?
And is there honey still for tea?' This
simple line from Rupert Brooke's poem
'The Old Vicarage, Grantchester' has
immortalised a small 19th-century
orchard and tea garden on the outskirts
of Cambridge. More contemporary
fame comes from Pink Floyd and Roger
Waters' 'Grantchester Meadows' from
the Ummagumma album of 1969.
Grantchester is a village on the River
Cam that is said to have the world's
highest concentration of Nobel Prize
winners. Students and tourists often
travel from Cambridge by punt to picnic
in the meadows or take tea at The
Orchard. In 1897, a group of Cambridge
students had persuaded the owner of
Orchard House to serve them tea in its
apple orchard, and this became a regular
practice. Lodgers at Orchard House
included Rupert Brooke, who later moved
next door to the Old Vicarage. More
recently the house became the home of
the Cambridge scientist Mary Archer and
her husband, Jeffrey Archer, Baron Archer
of Weston-super-Mare. The footpath to
Cambridge that runs beside Grantchester
Meadows is nicknamed the Grantchester
Grind, accessed by the stile shown here in
Glynn's soporific scene. Further upstream
is Byron's Pool, named after Lord Byron,
who is said to have swum there.

⌃ The Backs
2005 – 72 x 15 cm

The Cambridge Backs is the name given to a stretch of reclaimed land that runs along the rear of the riverside colleges, depicted here by Glynn in all its splendour. The area provides stunning views throughout the year, and is covered with a blanket of daffodils and crocus in the spring. The land forming The Backs is located to the east of Queen's Road, where several colleges back on to the River Cam, their grounds covering both banks of the river. The area, from Magdalene Street Bridge in the north to Silver Street Bridge in the south, consists of the rear grounds of Magdalene College, St John's College, Trinity College, Trinity Hall, Clare College, King's College and Queens' College. Historically, much of the land has been used by the colleges for grazing livestock or growing their own fruit.

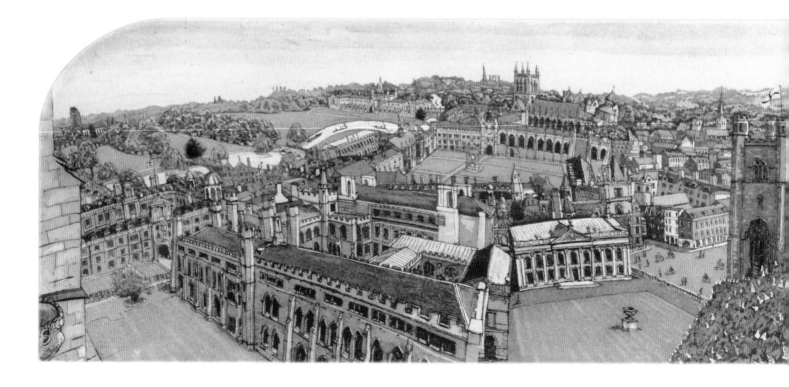

▼ From King's College Chapel
2005 – 72 x 15 cm

Virtually the entire City of Cambridge can be seen here at a single glance. Viewed from King's College Chapel, Glynn captures a mighty vista of classical architecture and seats of learning. The Chapel itself is one of the most famous buildings in the city and in the country, representing a magnificent example of late Gothic architecture. It was started in 1446 by King Henry VI, and took more than a century to build. It has the largest fan-vault ceiling in the world, and some of the finest medieval stained glass found anywhere in Europe.

◄ Punting

1996 – 37 x 13 cm

Centred on Clare College Bridge over the River Cam, Glynn's picture represents a typical summer scene in Cambridge, where tourists are lured on to the fleet of student-operated punts for a memorable outing. The River Cam enters Cambridge from the south west of the city, heading north past many of the historic colleges along the open area known as The Backs. After passing St John's College, it turns sharply and runs east, passing the weir at Jesus Green and the boathouses alongside Midsummer Common. Clare is the oldest of the current bridges, built in 1639–40 by Thomas Grumbold. All of its contemporary structures were destroyed by Parliamentarian forces during the English Civil War, in order to make Cambridge more defensible. There are many stories to explain the missing section of the globe second from the left on the south side of the bridge. One is that the builder of the bridge received inadequate payment, and in return removed a segment of the globe. Another is that complete bridges were subject to a tax at the time of building. By leaving off a segment, the bridge was incomplete and therefore tax exempt.

Like the people on the bridge in Glynn's print, from this vantage point you can enjoy the not infrequent spectacle of a marooned 'punter' with his pole stuck in the mud.

ʌ Ferry Path
2013 – 19 x 33 cm

This quaint, largely residential street in a tranquil part of North Cambridge is very familiar to Glynn, being part of the 'stomping ground' of his youth. The quiet, car-free path accommodates The Old Spring public house and, like so many Glynn Thomas scenes, it is also home to at least one cat – take a look at the house neighbouring the sunflowers. Along Ferry Path, a terrace of around 30 cottages was built from 1844. Each has a well-tended garden, and the white cat is clearly a proud resident of this desirable and picturesque byway to the River Cam. Ferry Path forms part of the Chesterton conservation area, of which there are 11 in Cambridge. Chesterton is a popular suburb located around a mile to the north east of the city centre. The early historic buildings that are grouped around the waterfront recall the historic significance of waterborne

transport to the area, with grand houses built in the vicinity and the Green Dragon Inn serving users of the crossing point remembered in the name Ferry Path. In fact, there were several ferry services operating during the years before bridges began to span the river in this part of Cambridge. Among the numerous ferries crossing the Cam from the Middle Ages were the 'old ferry', which was particularly profitable during the Stourbridge Fair in the 1550s and 1560s. By the middle of the 18th century, this ferry was run from the Green Dragon Inn. Boat-building flourished in the 19th century, when many people were employed in that trade along Water Street. Private boatyards, located immediately adjacent to the river, disappeared gradually as various of the University's rowing clubs established their own boathouses. There are excellent

views of the boathouses along the river, and across to Stourbridge Common, from the current pedestrian/cycle bridge located at the southern edge of the area. On the opposite bank of the river, and seen clearly in Glynn's print, is the part-16th-century inn The Fort St George In England, to give it its full name. This popular timber-framed pub with its ancient panelling is situated on the edge of the much-loved Midsummer Common; and also overlooks the Cam which, as always, is busy here with university rowers. The old sprawling building appears much larger from the outside than it seems from within. It also boasts an extensive garden on two sides, and a substantial covered area overlooking the common. During local events such as the busy Midsummer Fair, the pub often closes to avoid trouble.

∧ Cambridge Buskers
1990 – 6 x 9 cm

Busking in Cambridge is such a popular means of supplementing income and demonstrating talent that the city has its own code of conduct for these street performers. The 'Busker's Code' states that music or voice shall not be so loud that either can be heard beyond a distance of 30 metres. Buskers shall not occupy any pitch for more than one hour at a time and shall not return to the same pitch again on the same day. Street musicians are advised not to set up a pitch within 50 metres of another busker. They aren't allowed to obstruct the flow of pedestrians in the street, and they must not solicit contributions or offer merchandise for sale. Busking also should not start before 8am, but this rule is probably wasted on Cambridge students!

‹ Cambridge Lanterns
1999 – 24 x 63 cm

This scene was drawn from St John's Chapel, and Glynn captures a pigeon's-eye view of Cambridge rooftops and lanterns, looking towards Trinity College. The ornamental cupolas, or lanterns, let light through into the dimly lit buildings below. As well as St John's lantern, the picture also features Trinity Great Court, Clare College and King's College. Look closely and you can just make out Queens' College Mathematical Bridge at the top.

⌃ Cambridge Mill Pools
2013 – *27 x 27 cm*

Punts, pubs, rivers and restaurants are key ingredients of this watery scene. In the top left corner, a quiet stretch of river meanders towards Grantchester; while at the bottom right the Granta pub attracts locals and tourists in their thousands. More than one punt hire station is visible in Glynn's print, as the Granta has its own well-used facility. The one shown at the bottom left is also a popular meeting point for students, who gather for drinks at The Mill pub and

celebrate graduation out on Laundress Green, which runs alongside the river Cam. If they get hungry and want a change of scenery, the impressive stone building found top centre in the print is currently an Italian restaurant, boasting great views from the old watermill that still retains a wooden waterwheel inside the building. From its terrace, diners can watch in amusement as the punts attempt to turn around as they reach the wide end of the river. Top right in Glynn's picture is the

distinctive Malting House on Newnham Road, situated opposite the Granta on the corner of Malting Lane. It belongs to Darwin College and provides student accommodation in its 11 rooms. The Malting House School (also known as the Malting House Garden School) was an experimental educational institution that operated from 1924 to 1929. It was set up by the eccentric and, at the time, wealthy Geoffrey Pyke in his family home and was run by Susan Sutherland Isaacs.

➤ Peterhouse

2008 – 29 x 20 cm

Peterhouse is the oldest of the constituent colleges of the University of Cambridge, founded in 1284 by Hugo de Balsham, Bishop of Ely, on its current site close to the centre of the city. It is a charitable institution, dedicated to 'the pursuit of excellence' in education, religion, learning and research, and is also the smallest Cambridge college, housing an intellectual community of some 45 Fellows, 260 undergraduates and 110 graduate students. The college was the first in the university to have electric lighting installed (and only the second building in Britain, after the Palace of Westminster) when Lord Kelvin provided it for the Hall and Combination Room to celebrate the college's 600th anniversary in 1883–1884. Peterhouse's main site is on Trumpington Street, to the south of Cambridge city centre, while the main part of the college is just to the north of the Fitzwilliam Museum, with its grounds running behind the museum. The area closest to Trumpington Street is referred to as First Court. It is bounded to the north by the Burrough's Building, to the east by the street, to the south by the Porters' Lodge and to the west by the Chapel, built in 1628 when Matthew Wren (Christopher Wren's uncle) was Master. Old Court lies beyond the Chapel cloisters. To the south of the court is the dining hall, the only college building that survives from the 13th century.

◄ Cambridge Folk Museum
1982 – 10 x 12 cm

This quaint museum in its 17th-century, timber-framed building was established in 1936 by leading members of the town and university in order 'to interest the ordinary citizen in aspects of local social life which are fast disappearing in Cambridgeshire'. Originally the White Horse Inn, the building has nine room settings, displaying such intriguing objects as moles' paws carried to prevent rheumatism, and glass 'Witch Balls' hung in the window to trap the reflection of any witch peering in.

◄ St Bene't's
1982 – 10 x 12 cm

This ancient parish church in Cambridge dates back to around 1020, when King Canute was on the throne. In 1352 the Guild of Corpus Christi, based at the church, founded Corpus Christi College. Thomas Hobson (of 'Hobson's Choice' fame) is buried in an unmarked grave in the chancel. Michael Ramsey, later Archbishop of Canterbury, was vicar at St Bene't's in 1938. By the 13th century, the church bell was used to summon students to special lectures and to examinations.

▼ St Ives
2005 – 12 x 27 cm

Formerly known as Slepe, in the old county of Huntingdonshire, this ancient riverside market town was subsequently named after the Persian Bishop St Ivo. St Ives, now within the county of Cambridgeshire, stands on the River Great Ouse and is world famous for the Chapel on the Bridge. For almost a thousand years, the wide centre of St Ives, now known as Market Hill, has hosted some of the largest public markets in England. Many years ago these markets included livestock, and for a time were some of the biggest of their kind. Today street markets still fill the town centre on Mondays and Fridays. Swans dominate the foreground of Glynn's picture, and are a constant presence on the river by the bridge. Anyone visiting should make sure to take a spare sandwich…

◄ Ely
2005 – 33 cm diameter

The 'Ship of the Fens', the magnificent Ely Cathedral dominates the landscape around this medieval city. It also dominates Glynn's etching, which highlights the flat, open landscape surrounding Ely. Founded in 673 when Princess Etheldreda, daughter of Anglo-Saxon King Anna, adopted Christianity and formed a convent near Cratendune, Ely's original abbey was destroyed in 870 by Danish invaders and not rebuilt for more than 100 years. Parts of the present cathedral date from 1081, with sympathetic restoration taking place between 1845 and 1870 by the architect George Gilbert Scott. Ely Cathedral has been voted in The Times as 'one of the top 20 must-see buildings in the UK'. Ely was also home to Oliver Cromwell.

▼ Ely Reflections
2005 – 18 cm diameter

Ely Cathedral here forms the backdrop to a more natural scene of swallows hunting over water on the outskirts of the city. Surrounding Ely, the peat-black fens reclaimed from their natural marsh state are criss-crossed by rivers and drainage channels. Major rivers, including the Witham, Welland, Nene and Great Ouse, feed into the fens. The Great Ouse actually flows through the south-eastern boundary of the city. The most important wetland habitat close to Ely is the National Trust's Wicken Fen, Britain's oldest nature reserve. It is managed traditionally by sedge cutting and peat digging, and is now home to 29 species of mammal, more than 200 species of birds, 1,000 types of moth and butterfly, 1,000 species of beetle, and 25 types of dragonfly.

Norfolk

Ranked fifth in area among the English counties, Norfolk attracts birds in their millions and tourists in their tens of thousands. Glynn holidayed here as a child and is still attracted by the wilderness of the north coast and its salt marshes, shingle spits and seaside towns. The City of Norwich is captured in all its glory, and Glynn even portrays the familiar skyline of Cromer.

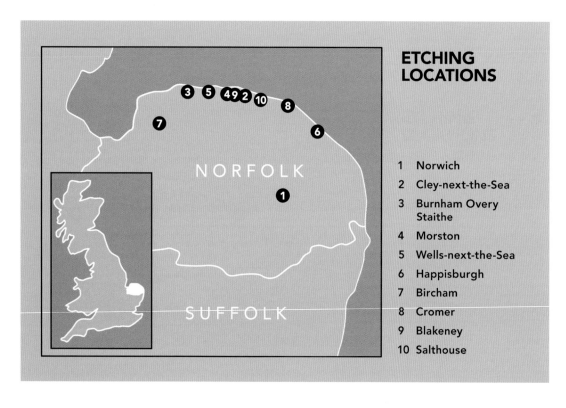

ETCHING LOCATIONS

1   Norwich
2   Cley-next-the-Sea
3   Burnham Overy Staithe
4   Morston
5   Wells-next-the-Sea
6   Happisburgh
7   Bircham
8   Cromer
9   Blakeney
10 Salthouse

➤ Norwich
1980 – 64 x 41 cm

Glynn's etching captures the majesty of an elegant and ancient city, featuring the spire of the Anglican cathedral, the Art Deco lines of the City Hall and the historic Pull's Ferry and Bishop Bridge on the River Wensum. Founded in 1096 and built using Normandy stone shipped over from Caen, the Anglican cathedral is one of the finest complete Romanesque buildings in Europe. Marked by a picturesque 15th-century water gate at Pull's Ferry, a canal from the River Wensum was dug by the Normans to allow stone for the cathedral to be ferried as close to the construction site as possible. The Caen stone was brought by sea from France and shipped up the river. Tombland, also featured in Glynn's print, is located in front of the cathedral and was once the Saxon marketplace in Norwich. From Tombland, two gateways lead to Norwich Cathedral: Erpingham Gate, built around 1420; and Ethelbert Gate, named after St Ethelbert, a young king of East Anglia who was killed in AD794. Norwich Cathedral Close, one of the largest in England, extends to more than 44 acres. It contains a mixture of 18th- and 19th-century terraces, plus more distinctive Dutch gables. The market, seen in the picture, is the largest Monday-to-Saturday open-air market in the country.

◄ **Cley-next-the-Sea**
2003 – 19 x 33 cm

Nowadays a mile from open water, Cley was once a major port, importing and exporting a variety of goods. The main trade today is tourism, with the village a magnet for bird-lovers and artists. The 18th-century windmill is beautifully preserved and provides B&B accommodation, with rooms looking out on to the marshes and shingle beach beyond. The area between the village and the sea is an Area of Outstanding Natural Beauty. In Glynn's picture, the mill is being circled by swifts, the other summer visitor that mobs the village. He cleverly avoids showing the snake of slow-moving traffic that clogs the main road throughout the tourist season.

⌃ **Avocets**
2009 – 12 x 7 cm

Looking back towards Cley-next-the-Sea and its windmill from the neighbouring town of Blakeney, Glynn here depicts the famous black and white wading birds that are the subject of the logo for the RSPB. Avocets have become a major success story in British bird conservation, having come back from the brink of extinction to form large colonies in places such as Cley and Blakeney. They enjoy the saltmarsh and winding creeks, striding through the muddy shallows, sweeping with their upturned beaks to capture aquatic insects, crustaceans and worms.

◄ **Burnham Overy Staithe**
2009 – 29 x 20 cm

A mill, mud, birds and boats are the main
features of Glynn's etching, and reflect
pretty much the scene at this attractive
North Norfolk hamlet. Forming one of
many 'Burnhams' in the area, this is Nelson
country, home of Britain's greatest naval
hero. Burnham Overy lies between the
larger village of Burnham Market to the
west, and Holkham to the east. Burnham
Thorpe, the birthplace of Horatio Nelson,
lies one mile to the south east. According
to various letters and documents, Nelson
at the age of ten learnt to row and sail a
dinghy at Burnham Overy Staithe, two
years before joining the Navy. Between
Burnham Overy Staithe and the sea, the
river spreads out into numerous tidal
creeks cutting through the salt marshes,
and finally reaches the sea by passing
though the fronting sand dunes at a gap
known as Burnham Harbour. Small boats
can reach Burnham Overy Staithe through
this gap and creek. Today, Burnham Overy
Staithe and the associated harbour is a
major recreational sailing centre.

⌃ Happisburgh
1991 – 6 x 9 cm

Famous as a disappearing Norfolk village, due to coastal erosion, the candy-striped lighthouse remains the dominant feature of Happisburgh, sited midway between Cromer and Great Yarmouth. The wooden sea defences built in the late 1950s have been failing for many years, and large chunks of the sandy cliffs fall regularly into the sea, with the loss of footpaths and even buildings. Happisburgh Lighthouse is the oldest working light in East Anglia, and the only independently run lighthouse in Britain. Built in 1790, originally one of a pair, the tower is 85 feet high and the lantern is 134 feet above sea level. Saved as a working light by the local community, it is maintained and operated entirely by voluntary contributions. Equally prominent in Glynn's picture is the nearby 15th-century church of St Mary. In 1940, a German bomber released a trapped bomb during its return to Germany, and the shrapnel can still be seen embedded in the aisle pillars of the church.

➤ Ebb Tide
2009 – 42 x 9 cm

Walking the concrete causeway from the town at Wells-next-the-Sea towards the beach, lifeboat station and beach huts provides a view of the dozens of boats stranded by the tide on the mud of this once important port. Wading birds scuttle among the sailing boats, fishing vessels and dinghies, probing the damp mud for insects and crustaceans. Wells has been a port for at least 700 years, and was at its peak in the middle of the 19th century, when the quay was built. The primary trade was the import of coal, timber and salt, and the export of corn, barley and malt for breweries. An impressive feature of the quayside featured in Glynn's picture is the large granary building with its distinctive overhanging gantry. Built in 1903, the granary has now been turned into luxury flats with magnificent views of the harbour.

◄ **Morston Quay**
2009 – 29 x 20 cm

In the height of summer, the myriad small boats in Glynn's picture are joined by long, snaking queues of tourists waiting their turn to board trips out to the seal colony at Blakeney Point. Fleets of locally operated open boats haul visitors out to the sand banks and shingle spits to view the basking seals and colonies of terns. The National Trust visitor centre dominates Glynn's etching. It is the official centre for the Blakeney National Nature Reserve, and a good staging point for walkers on the Norfolk Coast Path that provides wonderful access to the vast acres of saltmarsh and the thousands of birds that feed there.

^ Bircham Mill

2003 – 13 cm diameter

Towering over Norfolk's undulating fields, Bircham Windmill is a fine specimen of a functioning corn mill, looking much the same today as it did a century go. Open to the public, it affords panoramic views over the North Norfolk countryside, as well as grinding the grain to produce flour for the on-site bakery and tearoom. Visitors can climb the five floors up to the fan stage and, on windy days, watch the sails and the milling machinery in action. Here, in one of Glynn's famous 'fisheye' views, the mill's unspoilt surroundings are captured, as are the swallows and swifts that are almost as plentiful as the summer tourists.

>> Cromer

2003 – 26 x 44 cm

Crabs, the pier and the church are perhaps the most memorable features of this Norfolk coastal town, and all play a part in Glynn's etching. Cromer was 'discovered' in the 18th century by well-to-do travellers as a watering place, growing only slowly at first due to its remote location, but gathering pace when the railway arrived in 1877 to connect the town with London. By the 1890s, Cromer was fashionable and many fine residences were built. In 1900, a new pier was erected and the promenade was lengthened and enhanced. The town's reputation for crab fishing is unrivalled, and you can still watch the crab boats arrive every morning with their catch, landed on the beach as there is no harbour. Glynn's picture hints at just how traditional the crab fishing fleet is, hauled from the sea by ancient tractors to deliver the famous Cromer crab to locals, town shops and restaurants, and even for export. At the end of the 19th century, the beaches to the east and west of the pier were crowded with fishing boats. Now, only around a dozen boats ply their trade from the foot of The Gangway on the east beach.

➤ Blakeney
2009 – 6 x 14 cm

Blakeney on the North Norfolk coast was
once an important commercial seaport,
like neighbouring Cley-next-the-Sea, and
was still active until the early 20th century.
Areas of the village date back to the 14th
century, such as the old Guildhall and its
undercroft. Today the harbour is silted
up, allowing only small boats to navigate
their way past Blakeney Point into the
North Sea. Just two narrow streets
provide access to and exit from Blakeney
Quay, both clogged with tourist traffic
throughout the summer as visitors flock
to view the picturesque estuary or stay at
the Blakeney Hotel in the foreground of
the picture. Those keen to see the seals
at Blakeney Point are better off heading
for nearby Morston Quay, which provides
regular boat trips. Glynn had originally
considered the view 'down' Blakeney from
the church, but a brisk walk around to the
saltmarsh opposite the hotel provided him
with a much more effective perspective
looking 'up' the town, giving the viewer a
feel for the claustrophobic nature of the
narrow thoroughfare from estuary to the
main Cromer-to-Wells road.

▼ Norfolk Sunset
2009 – 62 x 19 cm

As you reach the last few huts on the long stretch of sand at Wells-next-the-Sea, shown here, you turn the corner and start heading for Holkham Beach, forming part of the Holkham estate. As suggested by the picture title, this is a particularly good spot to observe the Norfolk sunset, with nothing to spoil the view but miles of clean sand and the occasional stand of pine trees. It may be a long, hot walk from Wells town or from Holkham itself, but it is worth the trip.

▼ Blakeney Point
2009 – 8 x 22 cm

A popular tourist attraction by open boat from either Blakeney or Morston Quay, this three-mile spit of shingle and sand accommodates terns and seals in large numbers. Most people simply watch the seals from the comfort of their boat, while the seals return the compliment. You can, however, land and take a walk by the Old Lifeboat House shown in Glynn's print, now used by wardens and as an information centre. Blakeney Point is one of the best places in the UK to watch and study seals. The colony is made up of Common and Grey seals, and numbers around 500. The Common seals have their young between June and August, the Grey seals between November and January. The seals usually bask on the sandbanks at the far end of the spit. During the summer months you can usually spot Common, Sandwich, Little and Arctic terns.

⋀ Salthouse
2003 – 13 x 42 cm

The name of this popular North Norfolk coastal village comes from the once valuable commodity of salt, from which the word 'salary' is derived. The Domesday Book of 1086 describes it as a 'House for the storing of salt'. Salthouse is now famed for its unspoilt beauty and the thousands of birds attracted to the marshes. Some 66 hectares of coastal grazing marsh and salt-rich lagoons are managed as a nature reserve by the Norfolk Wildlife Trust. Lying between Walsey Hills and Kelling Hard, the marshes are of international importance for wildlife, particularly birds. Glynn manages to fit in a few familiar species such as avocet, curlew and oystercatcher, as well as geese forming a skein in the far left of the picture.

⌃ Wells-next-the-Sea
2009 – 24 x 63 cm

Beach huts and pine trees form the basis of Glynn's print. Both line the sand at one of Norfolk's most popular coastal resorts, the quaintly named Wells-next-the-Sea. The brightly coloured huts are some of the most expensive real estate in East Anglia, and can be found after a brisk walk from the bustling town. Wander for a mile and a half along the beautiful sandy beach and you'll end up in Holkham. Actress Gwyneth Paltrow walked across the very same stretch of sand during the closing scenes of 'Shakespeare in Love'. This is a designated Area of Outstanding Natural Beauty, allowing visitors to catch a glimpse of shore larks, ringed plovers, oystercatchers and terns during the summer. The name Wells derives from the many clear spring wells that were found in the area. The town became known as Wells-next-the-Sea in the early 1800s, to distinguish it from other places in Norfolk of the same name. In 1956, this became the town's official title. Located more than a mile from open water, the name nowadays may seem to be a slight exaggeration. In the late 16th century, however, the town benefited from much easier access to the sea, and was one of the major ports for the area. A handful of fishing boats still go crabbing, shrimping and whelking from the quay, which sits in front of a network of narrow streets, old alleys and yards, boasting some impressive Georgian and Victorian architecture.

England...

While London has often received the Glynn Thomas treatment, particularly on and around the River Thames, his range extends to Whitby in the north, Brighton to the south and even the Isles of Scilly at the farthest corner of the British Isles.

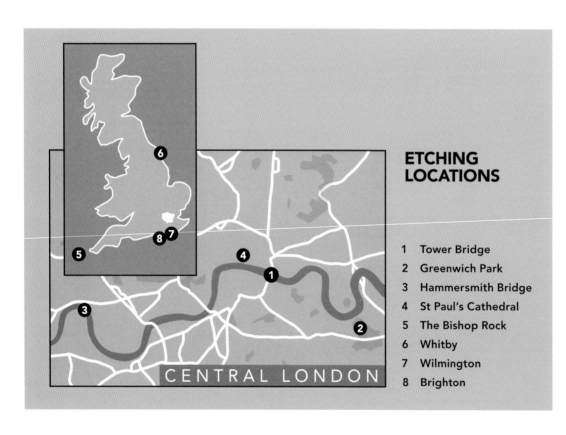

ETCHING LOCATIONS

1   Tower Bridge
2   Greenwich Park
3   Hammersmith Bridge
4   St Paul's Cathedral
5   The Bishop Rock
6   Whitby
7   Wilmington
8   Brighton

➤ **Tower Bridge**
1995 – 64 x 41 cm

The passage of a three-masted tall ship through the opened Tower Bridge will have been a sight to see. Glynn's view down the Thames shows us many other river crossings, including London, Southwark and Blackfriars bridges. None, of course, have the architectural splendour of Tower Bridge. London Bridge was originally the only crossing for the Thames. As London grew, so more bridges were added, but were generally built to the west, since the area east of London Bridge had become a busy port. In the 19th century, the East End of London became so densely populated that a new bridge became essential. In 1876, the City of London Corporation recognised the need, but had to face the challenge of a river crossing that wouldn't interrupt shipping movements. More than 50 designs were submitted for consideration; and, in October 1884, city architect Horace Jones, in collaboration with John Wolfe-Barry, offered the chosen design. It took eight years, five major contractors and the labour of 432 construction workers to build Tower Bridge. Once completed, it was the largest and most sophisticated bascule bridge ever built. Steam originally powered the pumping engines that raised the bridge, but today oil and electricity are used. This print forms part of the Museum of London art collection.

⌃ Greenwich Park

1999 – 33 cm diameter

From Canary Wharf to the London
Eye and Millennium Dome (now the O$_2$
arena), Glynn's etching of Greenwich
Park shows an awful lot of London.
Sir Christopher Wren's magnificent
Greenwich architecture is on display, while
the public are clearly enjoying the open
green spaces. The Park covers 183 acres
and is the oldest enclosed royal park. It is
situated on a hilltop with impressive views
across the River Thames to Docklands and
the City of London, between Blackheath
and the River Thames. Greenwich Park
provides a fantastic setting for several
historic buildings, including the Old Royal
Observatory, the Royal Naval College,
the National Maritime Museum and the
Queen's House.

∧   Hammersmith Bridge
1994 – 37 x 28 cm

Houseboats, smart houses and hostelries throng the banks of the River Thames in Glynn's view of Hammersmith Bridge. Even a Thames sailing barge has made a call, while rowers appear to be getting in some practice for the Oxford-Cambridge Boat Race. Construction of a bridge in this location was first sanctioned by an Act of Parliament in 1824, and work on site began the following year. It was the first suspension bridge over the River Thames, and was designed by William Tierney Clark. By the 1870s, the bridge was no longer strong enough to support the weight of heavy traffic, particularly when 12,000 people crowded on to it to watch the University Boat Race, which passes underneath just before the halfway point of its course. The current Hammersmith Bridge was designed by noted civil engineer Sir Joseph Bazalgette, and rests on the same pier foundations that had been laid for the original structure. The new bridge was built by the firm of Dixon, Appleby & Thorne, and was opened by the Prince of Wales on 11 June 1887.

Dome of St Paul's
2004 – 29 x 20 cm

While the dome of Sir Christopher Wren's masterpiece may dominate Glynn's picture, he introduces some other familiar landmarks for the more observant. Shakespeare's rebuilt Globe Theatre is on the far bank of the Thames, now reached by the Millennium Bridge over to the Tate Modern art gallery at Bankside power station. The present St Paul's is the fifth cathedral to have stood on the site since AD604, and was built between 1675 and 1710, after its predecessor was destroyed in the Great Fire of London. This was the first cathedral to be built after the English Reformation in the 16th century, when Henry VIII removed the Church of England from the jurisdiction of the Pope. Wren, the architect of St Paul's, was an extraordinary figure. Best known for his

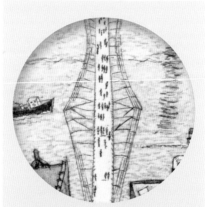

Early users of the footbridge were shaken up by the experience. It was prone to 'sway' when first opened, resulting in a two-year closure.

exceptional buildings, he was also an astronomer, scientist and mathematician. As an architect favoured by royalty and state, Wren's commissions ranged from the Greenwich Observatory and Greenwich Hospital to extensive work at Hampton Court and Kensington Palaces, as well as some magnificent buildings in Oxford.

∧ The Bishop Rock

2003 – 26 cm diameter

Looking through Glynn's 'fisheye' lens, the famous Bishop Rock lighthouse actually appears at the top of the image, reflecting its remote position off the westernmost tip of the Isles of Scilly. Comprising space for nothing more than the uninhabited 49-metre-high lighthouse, the rock acts as the barrier between the islands of Great Britain and the Atlantic Ocean. The original lighthouse was begun in 1847, and built from iron, but was washed away before it could be completed. The present building was finished in 1858. Bishop Rock is also the eastern end of the North Atlantic shipping route used by ocean liners in the first half of the 20th century, the western end being the entrance to Lower New York Bay. This was the route that ocean liners took when competing for the transatlantic speed record, known as the 'Blue Riband'.

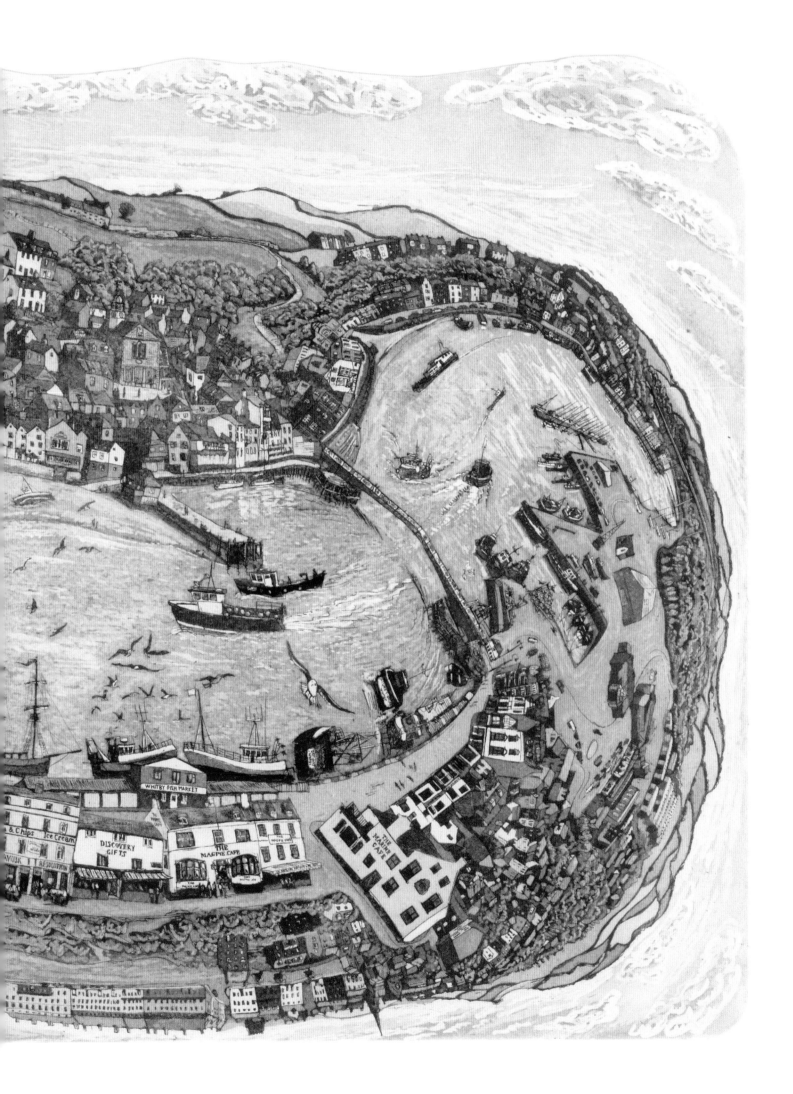

◀◀ Whitby

2007 – 36 x 60 cm

Dracula made his debut in the UK at Whitby, and must surely be among the figures featuring in Glynn's portrait of the Yorkshire coastal town. Old sailing ships and new fishing boats have skirted the lighthouse to dock at Whitby, in the shadow of the ruined abbey. St Hilda's Abbey was founded originally in AD657 by the Saxon King of Northumbria, Oswy as Streanshalh. In 867, the abbey fell to Viking attack, and was abandoned until 1078, when it was re-founded by Regenfrith, a soldier monk, under the orders of his protector, the Norman, William de Percy. The second monastery lasted until it was destroyed by Henry VIII in 1540. From the old town of Whitby, 199 steps lead up to the parish church of St Mary, whose churchyard on the town's East Cliff gave Bram Stoker the inspiration to write 'Dracula'. The fishing port emerged during the Middle Ages and developed important herring and whaling fleets, and was where Captain Cook learned seamanship. Tourism started in Whitby in Georgian times, and developed with the coming of the railway in 1839.

∧ Wilmington

1998 – 15 x 23 cm

There is a direct connection between this Sussex village and the subject of one of Glynn's most famous etchings, Honfleur in France (see page 115). In the late 1100s, a priory was built at Wilmington by the Abbot of Grestein from Honfleur. The church was constructed slightly later for the local peasants to use. Here, the famous 'Long Man' lurks in the background on the South Downs. Standing 226 feet high, he is cut in chalk and outlined with white bricks. He is believed to pre-date the Saxons, but even experts are uncertain of his exact age.

➤ Brighton

1995 – 64 x 41 cm

The author's birthplace, Brighton has had a chequered past. Glynn here shows the great folly of King George IV, the Royal Pavilion, plus the one remaining pier, once called Palace Pier, but now renamed Brighton Pier after the demise of nearby West Pier. The pebble-strewn beach is mobbed with summer tourists, and the picture shows the ancient shopping network called 'The Lanes'. Between 1800 and 1830, George, Prince of Wales, made Brighton the fashionable place to be, and lavished a fortune on his new palace, The Royal Pavilion, which was transformed into its exotic opulence in 1822 by architect John Nash. The Pavilion is surely one of the most eccentric buildings in the country. High society followed the Prince of Wales, and the obscure fishing village of Brighthelmstone established itself as a royal court second only to London. A building boom followed, and the architectural style that evolved became known as Regency. Major landmarks that identify the city today were built by the Victorians, such as the two piers, the aquarium, the magnificent avenues in Hove, the old Engineerium and the Clock Tower. In 2000, the Queen granted Brighton and Hove city status.

Brighton beach isn't known for its bird-watching, so what has the man with the binoculars seen? Surely not the naked lady picked out by the blue spot!

... and Beyond

Glynn's trek through the Himalayan region of Nepal was recorded in its own small book, but it is not the only international location to have caught his artistic eye. From rural France and the canals of Venice, to maritime New England and the High Andes, nowhere is immune.

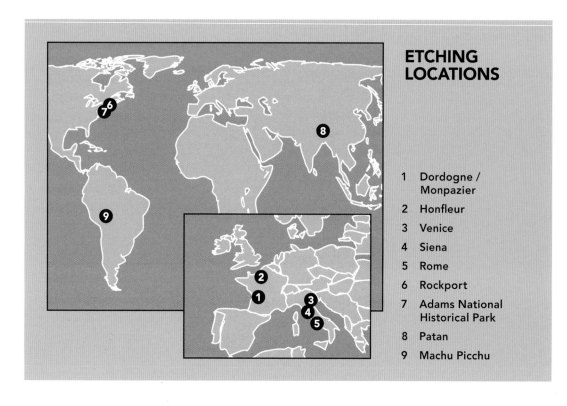

ETCHING LOCATIONS

1 Dordogne / Monpazier

2 Honfleur

3 Venice

4 Siena

5 Rome

6 Rockport

7 Adams National Historical Park

8 Patan

9 Machu Picchu

> **Dordogne**
> *1991 – 64 x 41 cm*

Dordogne is a départment in south-west France, located in the region of Aquitaine, between the Loire valley and the High Pyrénées. It is named after the great Dordogne River that runs through it. Shown here, Beynac is a small village spread along the northern bank of the river, which continues up the hill to the chateau perched above. Beynac is listed as one of the most beautiful villages in France. From the chateau, visitors can look down on a bend in the Dordogne River and on the charming village itself.

◀ Monpazier
1991 – 37 x 28 cm

Monpazier was founded in 1284 by King Edward I of England with the help of Pierre de Gontaut, Lord of Biron. It was only during the 14-year reign of King Charles V of France from 1366 that the bastide (fortified town) became definitively French. Measuring 400 metres by 220 metres, the town is quadrilateral in shape. Streets run parallel to the longest sides from one end of the town to the other, and are then crossed by four other streets to create rectangular compartments. The central Place des Cornières is surrounded by medieval and 17th-century houses. Unusually, all of Monpazier's houses were originally the same size and separated from each other by narrow side alleys to prevent the spread of fire. The square shown in Glynn's print is surrounded by houses whose ground floors form the arches of an arcade. The old market hall is intact, with its 16th-century timber roof frame supported by wooden pillars that are, in turn, mounted on blocks of stone.

Market day in Monpazier is clearly for more than just shopping: these two gentlemen appear to have enjoyed a very good lunch!

⌃ Honfleur
1983 – 29 x 20 cm

This depiction of a pretty Normandy town that has become a mecca for tourists and painters was awarded the Davys' prize for best print at the Royal Society of Painter-Printmakers' 1983 annual exhibition. The changing light along the River Seine has always attracted artists, among them great Impressionists such as Claude Monet and Eugène Boudin. Honfleur's Old Dock in particular must have been painted tens of thousands of times, each with a different sky as a backdrop. Glynn's own interpretation shows the unusual tall, narrow buildings along the dockside, reflected in the calm water. The town is on the southern bank of the estuary of the Seine across from Le Havre, and very close to the exit of the Pont de Normandie. Seen in Glynn's print is the ancient wooden church dedicated to Saint Catherine of Alexandria. The first nave is the oldest part, dating to the second half of the 15th century, constructed just after the Hundred Years War.

⌃ **Burano**
2002 – 26 x 14 cm
With its enchanting multi-coloured
houses, Burano is a popular tourist
destination on the Northern Venetian
Lagoon. The 3,000 inhabitants can take
the Canale Bisatto – Canale Carbonera –
Scomenzera San Giacomo's trail from the
small island to Venice. Some locals say
that each fisherman painted his house
a different colour so as to be able to
see it from a distance.

◄ **Hidden Venice**
1988 – 62 x 19 cm
This print of Glynn's is designed
to avoid the most obvious tourist
hot-spots of Venice, detailing instead
some of the lesser bridges and canals
'hidden' from the casual visitor.

⌃ Santa Maria dei Miracoli
2002 – 26 x 14 cm

This, the favourite church of Venetians, is also known as the 'marble church', and is one of the best examples of early Venetian Renaissance architecture. The main altar is reached by a series of steps. Santa Maria dei Miracoli was built between 1481 and 1489 by Pietro Lombardo to house a miraculous icon of the Virgin Mary.

➤ Venetian Bridges
2000 – 62 x 19 cm

Gondolas, canals and bridges are, unsurprisingly, the main content of Glynn's print. Venice boasts some spectacular bridges, but only four span the Grand Canal: dell'Accademia, degli Scalzi, the Rialto and the controversial new Ponte della Costituzione.

‹ Cats' Forum
1994 – 20 x 18 cm

While many of Glynn's prints feature a cat, none boasts as many moggies as 'Cats' Forum', where the City of Rome is clearly infested with felines of many sizes and colours. The cats have populated the Roman Forum in front of the Colosseum. The main entrance to the Roman Forum is midway along the Via dei Fori Imperiali, a wide road between the Colosseum and its Metro station and Piazza Venezia. Originally a marsh, the Romans drained the area and turned it into a centre of political and social activity. The Forum was the marketplace of Rome and also the business district and civic centre. There are clearly weighty issues of state for the assembled moggies to debate.

‹ Siena
1995 – 64 x 41 cm

Siena is an historic city in Tuscany and the capital of the province of Siena. The centre of the city has been declared a World Heritage Site by UNESCO, and it is one of Italy's most visited tourist attractions. The majority of the construction of Siena Cathedral (Duomo) was completed during the early 13th century, when the Piazza del Campo grew in importance as the centre of secular life. New streets were built to provide improved access, and it served as the site of the market. A wall was built in 1194 at the current site of the Palazzo Pubblico to reduce the risk of soil erosion. During the 10th and 11th centuries, the town grew to the east and later to the north, in what is now the Camollia district. Walls were built to surround the city, and a second set was finished by the end of the 13th century. Much of the city wall structure still exists.

⋀ Rockport
1987 – 27 x 40 cm

A coastal town and port in the US state of Massachusetts, Rockport is located approximately 25 miles north-east of Boston at the tip of the Cape Ann peninsula, surrounded on three sides by the Atlantic Ocean. Today Rockport is primarily a suburban residential and tourist town, but it is still home to a number of lobster fishermen and artists, the latter drawn by the endless power of the Atlantic. Rockport Harbor and Old Harbor, both near the centre of town, provide deeper water for larger boats to dock in. This provides ocean access for the town's fishing community. The highest point in Rockport is known as Pool Hill, which is surrounded by the town forest.

> ➤ **New England Farmstead**
> *1995 – 29 x 20 cm*

A portfolio of work set in New England is the result of a firm friendship between the Thomas family and the Bunces from New Hampshire. Barbara and Tom Bunce had originally been collectors of Glynn's work. Many years ago they took the Thomases under their wing, resulting in Tom taking Glynn on an amazing road trip through this spectacular part of the US eastern seaboard. This scene represents a composite 'view' of typical New Hampshire farmland and dwellings. The centrepiece is thought to be the retirement home of former US President John Adams and his wife Abigail. Adams, the second US President, retired to his farm called Peacefield, and lived in the Old House, which was built in 1731. The house was occupied by the Adams family from 1788 to 1927. The Stone Library (1873) next to the Old House has the Adams' collection of 14,000 books.

∧ Durbar Square Patan
1996 – 39 x 28 cm

Glynn's journey through Nepal was the subject of an earlier book, but the magnificent etchings produced from the trip are worthy of further acknowledgement here. This scene is of the Patan Durbar Square complex, situated in the centre of Patan city, also known as Lalitpur, which houses the residence of the former Patan royal family. The square and its surroundings are excellent examples of ancient Newari architecture. There are three main courtyards in the palace: Mul Chowk, Sundari Chowk and Keshav Narayan Chowk. Mul Chowk, the oldest, is at the centre of the square. Several sizes and styles of temple occupy the western part of the complex. Principal among these are Krishna Temple, Bhimsen Temple and the Golden Temple of Hiranya Varna. The Krishna Temple of red stone, which holds a commanding position in the square, was built in the 17th century and is thought to be the first to feature Shikara architecture.

⋀ **Machu Picchu**
2001 – 33 cm diameter

Machu Picchu stands 2,430 metres above sea level, in the middle of a tropical mountain forest. This spectacular 15th-century creation of the Inca Empire has an extraordinarily beautiful setting. Its giant walls, terraces and ramps seem to have been cut naturally in the continuous rock escarpments. Machu Picchu covers 32,500 hectares in the Peruvian Andes. As the last stronghold of the Incas and of great archaeological significance, it is one of the most important cultural sites in Latin America. The surrounding valleys have been cultivated continuously for well over 1,000 years. Machu Picchu also provides a secure habitat for endangered species such as the spectacled bear. Although known to the locals for centuries, the site only received international attention in 1911 when 'discovered' by the American historian Hiram Bingham. Since then, Machu Picchu has become a major tourist attraction. Most of the outlying buildings have been rebuilt in order to give visitors a better idea of what the structures looked like originally.

Flora & Fauna

*Cats have always been an important part of the Thomas household
and make frequent appearances in Glynn's work. A nature lover from childhood,
he is more than happy to tackle frogs and flowers, birds and trees …*

➤ Spring
1988 – 37 x 28 cm

⌃ Last Orders
2011 – 8 x 15 cm

➤ Pond
1990 – 9 cm diameter

◄ **Catortionist**
2010 – 13 cm diameter

◄ **Catortionist**
2010 – 13 cm diameter

⋀ **Love**
2012 – 11 x 7 cm

⋀ **Long-tailed Tits**
2012 – 14 x 10 cm

Glynn Thomas

∧ **Midsummer**
1991 – 11 x 17 cm

➤ **Frog March**
1991 – 6 x 10 cm

Index

Back cover **Wandlebury.** On the Gog Magog hills just south of Cambridge, Wandlebury is a haven for walkers. *2013 – 26cm diameter.*

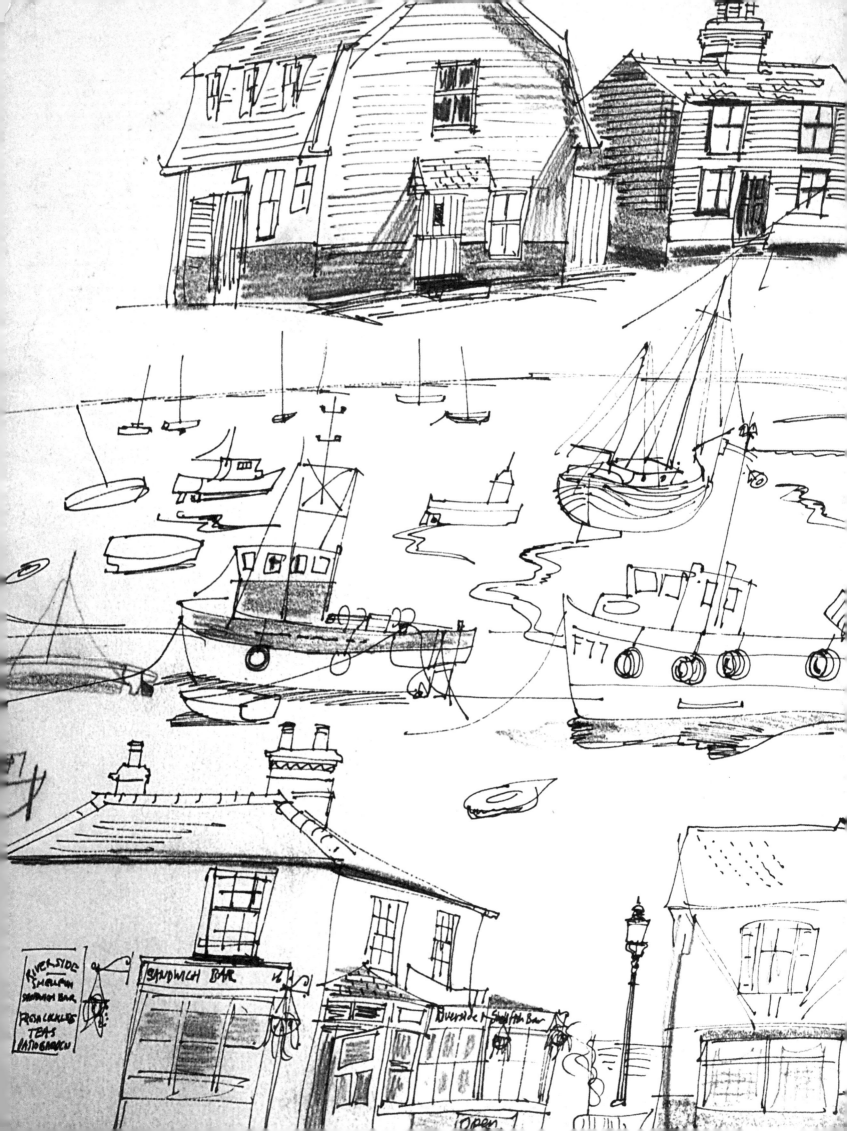